MY SECRET DIARY

D1332082

From Swaziland to Neverland

MY SECRET DIARY

BUBBLES

JB
JOHN BLAKE

Published by John Blake Publishing Ltd,
3 Bramber Court, 2 Bramber Road,
London W14 9PB, England

www.johnblakepublishing.co.uk

First published in paperback in 2009

ISBN: 978 1 84454 913 9

British Library Cataloguing-in-Publication Data:

A catalogue record for this book is available from the British Library.

Design by www.envydesign.co.uk

Printed in Great Britain by CPI Bookmarque Ltd, Croydon, CR0 4TD

1 3 5 7 9 10 8 6 4 2

This book is a work of fiction. The author has imagined the thoughts and
actions of Bubbles and everyone he came in contact with in his life to date.
It does not purport to be a true or accurate account of the Bubbles story and
no inference to this effect should be drawn by anything in the author's work.

Papers used by John Blake Publishing are natural, recyclable products made
from wood grown in sustainable forests. The manufacturing processes
conform to the environmental regulations of the country of origin.

To dearest MJ, the King of Pop

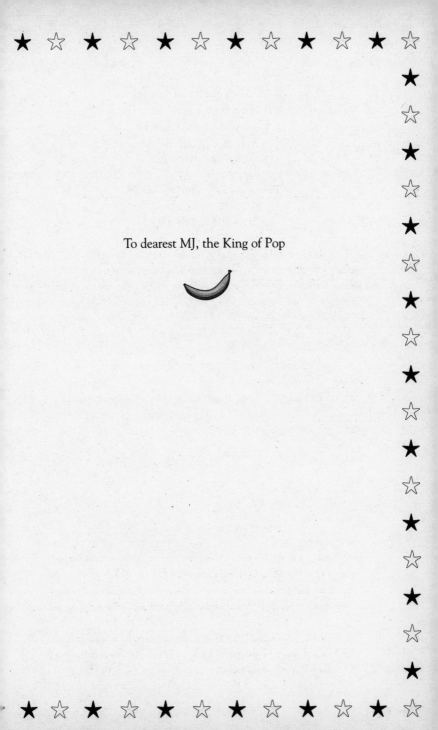

contents

Introduction

Life changed in 2002. After 17 years together, Michael and I were suddenly apart. The decision to go our separate ways was mutual. MJ looked around and found me a new home here at the Center. And what a home it is. Trees everywhere, bananas everywhere, apes everywhere: paradise for a chimp who's been, seen and done it all.

I've played the fame game with the best of them, but these days my needs are few. Gimme a few

bananas and a paintbrush and I'm hunky dory. My new addiction is painting (I have had much more dangerous addictions, as you'll discover) I mostly paint nudes of an old Chimpess I'm in love with. She's got something between her breasts that you never see between a young chimpess's: her navel. I'm no spring chicken myself. These days my back goes out more than I do, and that's fine by me. Life is very sweet here at the sanctuary.

When Michael died, I was devastated. Knowing he will never again visit me for a game of Monopoly has left a hole in my heart that will never be filled. But while I don't have Michael any more, I do have the wonderful memories of being around him during the best days of his life. Michael's end was tragic, for sure, but the Michael I knew was the opposite of that. He was kind, eccentric, and pure-hearted. In short, he was magic (but terrible at Monopoly, if I'm honest).

Like so many people – and a number of chimps

Introduction

– I'll miss Michael as long as I live, but when I
need to feel close to him I'll always have my diary
to flick through. I'm so glad to be able to share my
life with MJ with you. I do hope you enjoy it. If
you don't, then take a hike, bozo.

Bubbles

Center for Great Apes, Wauchula, Florida

October 2009

1983

Sunday 23 January

Just born. Thank God. I was totally through with hanging around inside Mum. A chimp needs to swing, man, and there wasn't much room where I just came from. Mind you, there's not an awful lot of room on the outside. I was hoping to pop out into the African wilds, but this place is about as far away from Swaziland as you could get. Mum and I are *inside*, for a start, and in a cage. There are a few

1

other chimps around, but they all look a bit moody. This is not what I'd bargained for.

Still, Mum told me not to worry – apparently I'm here to help scientists (whatever they are) further the cause of science (whatever that is) and that's a good thing. Sounds like dear mother's been brainwashed. If anyone wants my help they could start by making my surroundings a little plusher. Where's the swing rope I'd been dreaming of all these months. Where the devil am I?

Monday 24 January

Slept very deeply. Arriving in the world is exhausting business, and I must say I was pretty narked off when I was rudely awakened. I'd been dreaming of swinging through the treetops when a whistling sound woke me up. I rubbed my eyes and squinted up to find a very odd-looking creature in a white coat peering at me and smiling – must be

1983

one of these 'scientists' I've heard so little about. I wasn't impressed, and also unsure what the smiling was in aid of.

'Hello, Bubbles,' he said, staring at me. I looked around. Nope, definitely no bubbles to be seen. I wondered what on earth he wanted, and concluded he was quite possibly mad – if scientists do need help, I'm not sure if I'm the chimp for the job. 'Hello, Bubbles,' he repeated. Oh dear, I thought, the poor fellow's positively deranged. I looked back sympathetically, raised my eyebrows, shrugged and cuddled back into Mum.

The episode really rattled my cage, so to speak, and I slept the rest of the day. Mum too – I guess she's as zonked as me.

Tuesday 25 January

Told Mum about the bubbles man, and she burst out laughing – she was so beside herself that she didn't stop beating her chest and showing off her teeth for ten minutes. I was starting to worry that she was as crazy as him, but eventually she calmed down enough to speak. Suddenly, everything became clear. Horribly clear.

'You're Bubbles,' said Mum, still giggling. 'It's your name.'

Bubbles? BUBBLES! I've never heard anything so daft in all my life. So, I've only been alive three days, but, really, how utterly *patronising*. What is there about *me* that could possibly bring to mind a spherical envelope of liquid filled with air? Does my divine dark body resemble a globule? Do my sticky-out ears suggest a sphere? Is my face a shiny smooth ball that might go pop at any moment? No, no and no. I am in no way a bubble, let alone several of the dreaded things. And what an unsophisticated name – it's as if they're trying to imply I'm some kind of airhead. I'm 99.9 per cent human (and then some, in my opinion) and I deserve a bit more respect.

4

This chimp is reserved and intelligent, suave, savvy and shrewd (and pretty sexy with it), so why couldn't they just call me Richard or something?

Bubbles-schmubbles. I'm angry. Still, sticks and stones and all that. I suppose I'm simply going to have to rise above it.

Wednesday 26 January

Didn't rise above it.

In fact, I barely rose at all. Slouched in my cage all day and sulked. I needed some 'me time' to get over this bubbles fiasco. I was actually starting to feel a little better about it all (my name could have been worse than 'Bubbles', I'd reasoned – at least it wasn't 'fumes' or 'liquids') when Mr Scientist waltzed past with a sing-song 'Hello Bubs'. This sent me right back to square one. 'Bubs' wasn't a happy chimp. I frowned the meanest frown I could muster, then turned over and gave the grinning

white-coat a good look at my rear end. That wiped the smile off his face, and transferred it onto mine. Maybe I'll get over this after all.

Mum still really tired from the birth. Fair enough, but I'm *so* over sitting around all day while the old dear snores her head off. We're supposed to be bonding. I wish Mum would liven up a bit. This place is bor*ing*.

None of the other chimps have spoken to me yet. I try to say hello between cages, but they keep blanking me. Well, *excuse me* for having some manners. Not that I'm desperate to talk to them, of course. They seem like a right motley crew – I'm sure most of them are one banana short of a bunch, anyway.

Stonewalling creeps. Why the cagey silence?

Thursday 27 January

Mum woke me with a cuddle and told me she loved me. She'd been a little remote, if I'm honest, and I was starting to worry. God bless her, and shame on me for being so needy. Breakfast was Mum's milk, as always. Milk's nice, and all, and it's good of Mum to go the trouble (she has to sit there patiently while I guzzle for an eternity), but it's milk for breakfast, lunch and dinner. Five days in and I'm getting a little bored of the same old same old. Variety is the spice of life, right? Well, everyone else's meals look so much tastier. Bananas, nuts, figs and papayas appear to be where it's at – I bet those bananas really hit the spot. Hopefully I'll get my chops round one sooner rather than later. My stomach's rumbling as I write.

I asked Mum why the others weren't talking to me, and she said we'd have a chat in the morning. Good things happen to chimps who wait, don't they?

Friday 28 January

Not in my case they don't. Man, Mum laid some heavy shit on me today (not literally – that would

be crazy). We were on a walk around the concrete
courtyard (lucky us) while our cages were being
cleaned, when Mum took me aside.

'We need to talk, my darling,' she said, taking
my hand in hers.

'I'm all ears, Ma. Hit me with it.'

'When I said you're here to help science, I was
telling you the truth. But not the whole truth. I
didn't want you to hear about this on the ape-
vine, which is why I asked the others to keep
quiet until I'd explained everything. These
scientists use us chimps to test out cosmetics –
human luxuries like make-up and perfume. They
need to check the products are safe for humans.
We have no choice but to play ball, and it's the
last thing I want for my son. I'm afraid this is
your lot, sweetheart. I'm so sorry.'

I could hardly believe my oversized, but rather
endearing, ears. I was flabbergasted. The sadness in
Mum's eyes was heartbreaking – suddenly I realised

8

1983

the pain she'd endured for years. This was no life for a chimp, but she'd put up and shut up along with the rest of them. Why?

'Oh Mum, surely it doesn't have to be this way,' I said, gazing around at the others in the courtyard. What a downtrodden bunch they looked.

'There's no way out,' she replied, a tear coming to her eye. 'Those who've tried to rebel have always been taken away. To where, we don't know. We just have to toe the line.'

'And what exactly do *I* get out of this line-toeing business?' I enquired.

Mum shrugged. 'Bananas, I s'pose. Once you're old enough. Apart from that, not much.'

I felt a surge of anger rising in me. Me, donning makeup? What do they think I am, a transvestite? I'm a red-blooded dude, ready for a life of testosterone-fuelled adventure, not make up and perfume. If anyone thinks I'm gonna sit around dolled up to the nines like a geisha girl, I've got news for them. Ritual humiliation or uncertain future – I know which one I'd choose.

What makes humans think they have the right? Bugger science.

Count me out, for this chimp ain't playin' ball. Not for all the bananas in the whole world. Ape-solutely not.

Saturday 29 January

Had a weird dream last night. I was on a lawn next to a huge house, swinging away on a rope hanging from a huge tree. Surrounding me were more bananas than I could possibly eat, an embarrassment of yellow and black in huge piles. A man appeared. A very strange man with a big grin on his face. Thin, and clad in black leather, he wore white socks and a glove on one hand (obviously no scientist, then) and had a funny little nose. As he came closer, I noticed his face

was covered in make-up. This was one out-there dude, but he seemed friendly enough.

'Hey, Bubs,' he said in a high-pitched voice. 'Wanna hear a joke?'

I nodded as he threw me a banana.

'Why do monkeys have big noses?' he said, smiling as I peeled my banana. 'Because they have big fingers.'

I woke up laughing. It was still early, and everyone was asleep. What a trippy dream! Yesterday's chat about bananas and makeup must have messed with my mind. But what about the funny guy, what was that all about? Maybe it was a premonition or something, who knows?

Sunday 30 January

Jeez, this place is seriously depressing. Everyone sits around doing crap all. Picking one's toes is about as exciting as it gets. As for the science, nobody's whipped out the mascara yet. I'm starting to wish they would – so long as they don't bring it near me, you understand. A couple of the others smiled at me and said good morning, and left it there. Scintillating. Stuck inside as we are, we can't even talk about the weather.

Tuesday 1 February

Surprise, surprise, today was full of no surprises.

Ho-hum, there's always dinner to look forward to. An aperitif of milk, followed by a light milk starter, will leave room for milk for main course. I know a minute on the lips is a lifetime on the hips, but sod it, I'm gonna have some milk for dessert. I'm comfort eating.

Wednesday 2 February

Skipped breakfast. Last night's meal was a real blow out. Felt splendid for it though, and slept like a baby. Just as well, 'cos that's what I am.

Decided it was time to liven things up a bit. Mid-morning, I stood up, cleared my throat and addressed the masses.

'Okay guys and girls, everybody stop picking your toes and listen up,' I shouted. 'My name's Bubbles and I've got a line for you. Why do chimps have big noses?'

'I don't know, why *do* chimps have big noses?' they chorused.

'Because they have big fingers!'

The room fell apart. Chests were beaten, teeth were bared, and in an instant 20 chimps were jumping up and down in their cages making a right old racket. It's a funny joke, but not *that* funny, surely. Still it's the first time anyone's laughed since I was born, and I guess the sheer release of it caused the hysteria.

'Nice one, Bubbles,' shouted a grey old male. He looked like a real old timer. 'I'm Tinkles, by

13

the way. Nice to meet you, man.'

'You too,' I grinned, feeling blessed my name wasn't Tinkles. Then someone else piped up.

'Where do chimps get their hair cut?' chimed Biscuit, a rather dashing-looking fellow with hair in a striking centre parting (we're *so* stuck in the 1920s, us chimps).

Nobody knew where chimps got their hair cut.

'Vidal Baboon!' said Biscuit, deadpan. Everyone went nuts. Delila, a young female a couple of cages away, yelled that she thought she was going to wee herself, which only caused a third wave of mania.

The idea of Delila weeing herself made me laugh 'til I cried, but I didn't get the Vidal Baboon thing – maybe I'm too young. Didn't matter though, it was wonderful to see the gang happy for once.

The change in atmosphere is something to behold. Everyone's been chatting and swapping stories all day. Long may it last, I say. Maybe they're not such a bad bunch after all. Laughter is

the best medicine, and today it was *moi* who wrote the prescription. What a showman. Things are looking up.

Thursday 3 February

I wrote too soon. Things are definitely *not* looking up. Today was bad. Just after lunch (no prizes for guessing what gourmet treat I'd devoured) a scientist opened the cage, stuck his hand out, and motioned for me to come with him. I looked to Mum for help. 'You'll have to go with the man,' she said, forcing a smile (though I could tell she was holding back tears). 'Run along and be a good boy. Everything will be OK.'

Damn right it will, I thought, Ain't nobody gonna take Bubbles for a fool.

'This way, Bubbles,' said the man in the white coat. 'Time to go for a little walk to the laboratory.'

'*Yeah, I'll come with you,*' I screeched, '*but the*

buck stops there, sucker. *And what the hell's a laboratory anyway?*' He ignored me, took my hand and guided me out of the room. We walked down a long corridor into a brightly-lit room. Inside were several men in white coats (Why do they all dress the same? Talk about lack of imagination) surrounded by enough make-up to last Boy George a lifetime. (I nicked that line from Biscuit. Sounds kinda slick, though I've no idea who George is and why he needs to clarify that he's a boy. Sounds like a weirdo.)

'This is Bubbles,' said the man to the other men, who stared at me briefly before looking down at their clipboards. The manners on these cats! Not a great start, but, undeterred by their rudeness, I decided to break the ice. I screeched the Vidal Baboon joke at them (they didn't even look up, let alone laugh), then tried a bit of physical comedy. I clapped my hands three times, took a bow and grinned. And what did they do? Zilch.

Miserable bastards. And to think *I'm* the one doing *them* a favour. Despicable rudeness. But if that's the way they want to play it, fine. I can do nasty, no problemo. No more Mr Nice Guy.

I don't even know why they brought me here today. Instead of dolling me up like a streetwalker, they've gone and stuck me in a cage in the corner. From what they were muttering to each other, it seems I'll have to wait a couple of days and 'settle in' before they (try to) put my pancake face on. Suits me – waiting, that is, not the Max Factor.

What's more, there's a TV in the corner. Watched my first film, *Dirty Harry*. Now that's what I call a picture – not that I've seen anything to compare it with. Anyhow, Clint Eastwood sure knows how to control a situation. Loved the bit about asking yourself if you feel lucky, punk. In my case – though I'm no punk – it's a combination of yes and no: this place is getting me down but it'll be dinner time soon, which *is* lucky. Be good when Mum joins me for a feed.

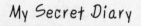

Friday 4 February

Starving. Mum didn't show last night. Some guy rocked up instead. 'Hello Bubbles,' he said with a smile. 'I'm Nigel. Got some dinner for you.'

With that, he gave me a bottle of milk. *Cold* milk. I held it in my hand and stared at Nigel in disbelief. Was this some kind of joke?

'Drink up,' he said encouragingly, his already infuriating smile still there. 'Lovely little milk for lovely little Bubbles.'

What the hell was he on about? This wasn't lovely; it was a downright insult. And I may be little, but I'm not *little*, thank you very much.

'*Piss off!*' I hissed, but nutty Nigel just kept smiling.

And then the penny dropped. These dudes don't understand a word I say to them, yet they talk to me as if I dig their language, *even though they think I don't*. But I do – I understand everything that comes out of their sorry-ass mouths. Time to test my theory out once and for all.

18

'Go on, get lost,' I continued, 'Go back to whatever rock you crawled out from, and take your freaky cold milk with you.'

'Nice milk for Bubbles,' winked Nigel. What a drip, he really didn't get it. The game was up. One-nil to Bubbles on the language score.

In the end, I threw the bottle into the corner of my cage and fixed Nigel with a killer cowboy stare. It was like something out of *Dirty Harry*, and my main punk Nige didn't look like he felt too lucky.

'Come on, Bubbles, drink up for me,' he said, hoping against hope.

Talk to the hand, sister, cause the face ain't listening.

Saturday 5 February

Being on hunger strike in a brightly lit room stuffed with eyeliner and no one to talk to is *not* my idea of a party. And *I'm* supposed to let them tart me up

19

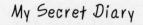
sooner or later. If only they knew what I've got in store for them, dear diary. If only they knew.

Sunday 6 February

My stomach's as empty as a cheerleader's head, but I'm not going to give in. Nigel turned up with more milk today, but I was having none of it. I wouldn't even look at him. Can't they understand I want *hot* dinners? I don't see why they can't bring Mum in and be done with it.

Monday 7 February

Where are you, Mum?

I love her, I miss her and I need some milk! I hope she's OK. Perhaps I upset her and that's why she hasn't come. Oh, God.

1983

Tuesday 8 February

Still no sign of Mum, but I'm over yesterday. I know she'd be here if she could. I've got to stay strong and stop doubting her.

Nigel left me the remote control for the telly, so hats off to him for that. I suppose the milk wasn't his idea, anyway. Maybe he's not so bad. I may be hungry, but at least I've got MTV.

Wednesday 9 February

Oh. My. God. TV is ace. Watched MTV all night long, and totally dug it. What a intriguing business music is. I mean, the tunes are great, but the popstars are nuts. Take Meat Loaf, for one. That guy's music is off the hook, but what's with the name? I'm guessing meatloaf is some sort of food, but it sounds totally gross. Surely there are nicer meals to name oneself after? Mind you, if I had to change my name to a dinner, my limited knowledge of the subject would leave me only one option, and Milk doesn't sound hip. I haven't eaten any yet, but calling yourself Bananas would be, well, bananas.

Thursday 10 February

I am in love. 110 per cent head-over-heels, knocked-for-six-never-look-back-I've-found-the-one besotted up to the eyeballs! And it's all down to one man – Nigel. I'm not in love with him – obviously – but I'm pleased to announce he's my best friend after what happened today.

I already had my nose turned up in anticipation of Nigel's dinner round (it saves going through the whole, 'Come on, Bubbles, drink your milk' farce), but I swiftly turned my hooter back down when I noticed what the dear man was holding. Rather than the usual bottle of milk, Nigel held a gorgeous-looking banana in his hand. For a second I thought I was hallucinating, but after a couple of

22

blinks and a pinch to the thigh, I knew it was the real deal. My chest tightened, I breathed in sharply, my mouth went dry. I gasped as he held out his eight-inch yellow masterpiece. Was it possible; could the banana really be for me? Not only *could* it be for me; it *was* for me.

'Got something for you,' beamed Nige. (Talk about state the bleedin' obvious, bless him).

I tried to play it cool, but to no avail. I couldn't control myself, and before I knew I'd done half a dozen backflips and was screaming like a banshee. Nigel laughed as he passed me my prize. *This* is what you get for going on hunger strike, I thought, the reward for being your own man and staying true to yourself. Well done me.

My hands shook a little as I gazed at the banana. Gently, I placed forefinger and thumb on its wonderful, firm stem, shuddered at the dull click of the skin breaking and delighted at the slick rip of the peel coming away.

The moment had come. It was time for my first nibble. I hesitated for a moment, gave Nigel a wink, and sunk my teeth into the soft pale flesh within.

It was heavenly; perfectly ripe and so exquisite that I groaned with sheer pleasure at every mouthful. The banana was down the hatch in seconds, and I could have demolished another 20, right there and then. But the banquet was not to be, for Nigel had only brought me one. Still, I'd fallen in love, and it's better to have loved and lost than never to have loved at all.

Lovely, gorgeous, wonderful Nige. To think I'd ever called him a fool. Dear God, please arrange it for my best friend (a total dude) to bring me another banana in the morning.

Friday 11 February

No such luck. Devastatingly, Nigel showed up empty handed this morning – unless you count the

bottle of milk he was clutching in his hand. I was as good as ready to cross him off the best friend list, when he offered me a lifeline.

'Would you like another banana?' asked Nige. What a dumbass question. Still, I jumped up and down excitedly (after all, Nige didn't know I could understand him, did he?), and for a second he looked at me funny (perhaps it dawned on him I *might* know what he was on about.)

'Well, here's the deal. You drink your milk and I'll bring you a banana,' said Nigel firmly as he plonked the bottle down in my cage. 'I've got a job to do, and your lack of cooperation isn't helping.'

I'd never had Nige down as a man who would drive a hard bargain, but his offer stopped me in my tracks. What a dilemma: how I longed for another beautiful banana, and how I loathed the idea of anything but Mum's lovely milk. Damn Nigel, he'd really got me between a rock and a hard place. Tempting as Nigel's offer was, I needed to think. Such delicate negotiations require a good poker face: my best Clint Eastwood stare would buy me some time to think. Nigel met my steady gaze.

'I don't think you understand me, do you?' he said, shaking his head and smiling. 'But if you do, consider my offer, OK?'

And with that, he left.

The milk can stay put. I'm not desperate.

Bubbles is cool.

Saturday 12 February

OK.

I'm desperate.

Stayed awake all night thinking about blasted bananas. Feel like I'm going crazy. If only I could talk to a psycho-bananalyst.

I can't believe just one piece of fruit has done this to me. Love sucks. Still, I ain't drinking that milk. No Sir. I've got to stay true to myself.

Sunday 13 February

Another sleepless night.

I have a banana for a brain, and I'm really not peeling – I mean feeling – well.

Keep staring at the milk. Maybe I should swallow my pride.

Monday 14 February

Pride swallowed.

Not a decision I took lightly, but after two sleepless nights I was starting to lose the plot. When Nigel showed up this morning, I grabbed the milk, pinched my nose and necked the lot in one.

Truth be told it wasn't as bad as I'd imagined (it wasn't half as good as Mum's, though). What a stubborn little chimp I am.

As promised, Nigel reappeared at lunchtime with not one, not two, but *three* large bananas. Wasted no time in dealing with that little lot.

Banana'd up to the eyeballs, I spent a blissful afternoon bugged out in front of MTV.

Tuesday 15 February

Finally worked out who Boy George is. Saw him singing 'Do You Really Want to Hurt Me' on MTV last night.

What a track.

And the answer's 'No', I wouldn't hurt bone in George's body (nor would I make him cry). But I'd happily give him some makeup remover – he's covered in the stuff. To think how many monkeys have suffered so the likes of him can dress up like girls. Now I see why he puts Boy before George.

The bananas keep on coming. That's my boy, Nigel.

Not that I'd ever call him Boy Nigel.

Wednesday 16 February

Woke up in a cold sweat after a terrible nightmare.

I was Boy Bubbles singing onstage with Bananarama. My face was dripping with foundation and pink lipstick, and I could hardly see for my false, mascara-clad lashes.

Terrifying, and so unlike me.

Nothing could get me to wear makeup (Correction: a lifetime's supply of my favourite yellow fruit might sway me, but what are the chances of that?) I think I should quit MTV for a while.

NBC's pretty funny, especially that *Cheers*. Sam's a dude, but how *thick* is Coach?! Reminds me of Nige. Nice enough, but one egg short of a fry up.

Nigel came by with four bananas. An extra special treat to thank me for being so good, apparently. Pleasure's mine, Nige, I thought, devouring them. Before leaving, he patted me on the head.

'Well done, Bubs,' he said fondly. 'I think you're ready now.'

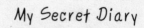
Ready for what? The only thing I'm ready for is bed, maybe an episode of *Cheers*. I *so* wish Sam would get busy with Diane. She's one hot banana. I'd always be ready for Diane.

Thursday 17 February

Cheers didn't disappoint (neither did my dreams of Diane). Just as well, for a trip along Big Let-Down Alley awaited me this morning.

To cut a long story short, Nigel has betrayed me.

To make a short story a little bit longer, it happened this morning when the creep should have been dishing up my brekkie. In he came as usual, bananas at the ready, but instead of handing the gear over, he placed my beloved friends just out of reach. Seconds later, two science bods strutted in. Nigel looked at me and smiled, but I could tell there was something fishy afoot.

'Good morning, Nigel,' said a scientist. 'Pleased

to see that Bubbles is finally ready for us.'

'Indeed,' replied Nigel, 'Bubbles has finally learned to behave himself, haven't you, Bubs?'

Suddenly it hit me. I'd been tricked. All those bananas and all that TV were about nothing more than buttering me up to be messed with. I didn't know whether to laugh or cry. I soon realised neither would do me any good, so did nothing of the sort. Instead, I got mad.

'*Why, you evil, lying, no good, low down piece of crud!*' I screeched at Nigel (I've already seen too many movies). '*If you think a few bananas and a couple of nights in front of the TV can buy me, you're sorely mistaken, my friend. Sorely mistaken, indeed!*'

And did they get the message? Did they understand one iota of what I was saying.

Negative.

I'll tell you what the dimwits did as I jumped and yelped in my cage: they *laughed*.

'Isn't he cute?' said one.

'*I'll cute you, asswipe!*' I shrieked.

'I think he's excited,' said the other.

'*Excited about how badly I'll whoop your butt if you
so much as lay a finger on me, punk!*'

And then it began.

'All you need to do is help the men and then
you can have breakfast,' said Nigel in what I can
only assume was meant to be a soothing voice.
'OK?'

I shrugged. Go along with them, Bubbles, then
choose your moment, I told myself. Play it cool,
just like Clint would, and keep your eye on those
bananas.

Nigel opened the cage and I hopped down to the
floor. I even put my hand up for Nigel to hold
(you've got to keep your enemies close). The traitor
took my hand and guided me across the lab to the
men. I took a seat on a high chair, and waited.

A box was placed on the table and opened. I
peered in. As I feared, it was rammed with makeup.

Boy George would have died and gone to heaven, there was so much of the stuff. Adrenaline shot through me quicker than a banana hit – my instinct was to run right away, but I kept my nerve.

One of the scientists walked round to my side and held me firmly by the arm. The other reached into the box and pulled out the star of a recent nightmare – mascara. My pulse quickened and a sweat broke in the small of my back. Carefully, the scientist coated a little brush with the poisonous black powder before leaning towards me, hand outstretched. I stared wide-eyed as the brush quivered before my face. This was it. My moment had arrived.

Quick as a flash, I took a perfectly-aimed bite at the hand of the weasel holding my arm (nothing serious, just enough to stun him), before letting out an almighty scream in Mascara Man's face.

As he winced, I snatched the brush from his hand, grabbed the makeup box, ran along the table,

mounted the fridge, and leaped onto to a high shelf.
I scuttled along it (deftly skipping over all manner
of funny little bottles) and reached my destination:
an air vent I'd had my eye on for a while.

I ripped off the cover, and popped the makeup
box through as easily as you'd post a letter. Mission
accomplished – nearly. There was one more thing –
the bananas.

Trouble was, Nigel was ahead of me and already
running towards my precious lovers. There was
nothing for it; I had to make a jump across the
room from the ceiling. I took a breath and leaped,
coming down next to my bananas just as Nigel
got there.

It was a stand off. We were both within grabbing
distance.

'Don't you *dare*,' shouted Nigel.

Yeah, right, I thought, and whisked the bunch
up. I took the time to stick my tongue out at Nige
and give him a little poke in the eye before

scuttling back to my cage and getting on with my (rather well-earned) meal. For this, I received no thanks. There was no need. It was the least I could have done for everybody.

Nobody said anything while I ate. The little trio seemed a little shocked, and not a word was spoken. They simply stared at one another dumbly.

Fascinating.

I was still on a high from my triumph, and couldn't have cared less.

Nigel did something pathetic before everyone skulked out of the door. He turned off my TV. How petty, I thought, reaching for my remote.

Feel good, but I don't fancy watching *Cheers* tonight. I need to rock out. I need music. It's been too long. I want my MTV.

Friday 18 February

I am very disturbed.

I'd only been watching TV for about ten minutes last night when a video came on that scared the living hell out me. *Thriller*, it was called, sung by some guy called Michael Jackson. What a freaky looking dude. I can't believe they let zombie werewolves like him make such terrifying pop songs. I was already shaking like a leaf by the end, and then that creepy, evil laugh totally finished me off. Hardly a thrill. Never again. I'm through with MTV. Back to *Cheers* for me.

I think Nigel and his cronies are trying to punish me after yesterday's incident. No one paid me a visit today. Understandable, I suppose – I really rocked the boat after all.

But what did they expect?

Nigel betrayed me and he got what he deserved – I don't call my behaviour violent; I'd call it self-defence. I felt triumphant yesterday, but now I just feel terrible. I don't trust these humans as far as I can throw them. And that's not very far at all.

36

1983

My cage is littered with banana skins. I think I'll
have to put them to good use...

Saturday 19 February

Woke up early, and carefully threw my banana
skins towards the door. Out of five, three landed
perfectly: splayed out, slippy side down. All I had
to do was wait, and not for long either.

Minutes later, Nigel stuck his head around the
door cautiously (perhaps I'd scared him, I don't
know). I gave him an encouraging wave to let him
know all is forgiven – which it most certainly isn't
– and my dear enemy stepped forward.

The broad smile on his face was soon replaced
with a confused, dumb look as his right foot
alighted on a banana skin which sent him and his
milk flying.

How I laughed.

I'd really got him, and he didn't look too pleased.

His cheeks flushed red, and he looked like he was about to explode.

'You *horrible* little beast,' he yelled as he stood up. 'Who on earth do you think you are? I bring you food and bananas and this is how you repay me?'

Damn right, buddy.

Sunday 20 February

Triumph at last. It seems they've finally got the message that Bubbles ain't playing ball. Nigel came in this morning, and glared at me.

'OK, Bubbles,' he said sourly. 'Let's go.'

It was time to return whence I'd come. As I skipped back down the corridor, I felt like a soldier returning unscathed from the war. The odds had been stacked heavily against me, but my steely reserve not to let the bastards get me down had won the day.

And what a hero's welcome I received.

The door to the chimp room flew open, and everyone cheered.

'Bubbles!' gasped Delila, 'You're alive.'

'Of course I'm alive, princess, you didn't think they could get rid of me that easily, did you?'

'Actually, yes,' she said, gasping some more. 'Many a chimp has been taken that way and never returned.' Looking at her innocent, admiring eyes, I suddenly realised what a cute little peach Delila was, and felt a strange, but not unpleasant stirring – I suddenly wanted to be near her. *Very near*. But it was neither appropriate (my urge involved activities I wouldn't want Mum to witness) nor possible (she was in a cage), and I did all I could to push my pangs aside.

Biscuit winked at me and smiled as I brushed past his cage, and Tinkles beamed. 'Welcome back, Bubbles,' he whooped. 'Boy, have we missed you!'

I glided through the room like royalty, and then suddenly I was standing in front of the most familiar cage of all – dear mother's.

It was an emotional reunion. Let's just say Steven Spielberg should have been there. Tears of joy flowed from Mum's loving eyes, and even I shed a tear. Not very Clint Eastwood of me, I know, but I'm only human (well, nearly). Being back with Mum was such sweet relief, and all I wanted to do was to hold her and get some decent milk down me. But there was something I had to do first.

'OK guys,' I piped up. 'Here's one. Why don't bananas snore?'

'Tell us, Bubs,' replied the room.

'Because they don't want to wake up the bunch.'

It floored them of course. The showman was back.

My work is done. Now it's time for some milk and a good sleep. It's wonderful to be back with Mum, but I already feel guilty about something: I miss my TV and – worse still – I'm craving bananas.

1983

Monday 21 February

Didn't have much time to myself today. Had a crowd to please.

Everyone was desperate to hear my tale of triumph against the enemy, and without hesitation I modestly recounted the trials and tribulations of the last three weeks. The crowd 'oohed' and 'aaahed', laughed and cried, and every pause was greeted by 'More, tell us more!' until I finally concluded my story to rapturous applause. I took several bows – praise for my daring defiance of the rules was heaped upon me from all, except one person: Mum. Once the commotion had died down, I noticed her slouched in the corner of the cage. Her eyes were watering and she looked angry.

'What's up, Mum?' I said, settling down next to her.

'I'll tell you what's up,' she said. 'You went against everything I told you, tried to be a hero and landed yourself in a whole heap of trouble. Just because

41

you're back here, it doesn't mean you're safe. Chances are they'll try again, and if you keep up your nonsense a second time, you won't be coming back.'

'But Mum...' I stammered.

'But nothing. I've had enough of your act. Next time you'll do as you're told, understand?'

I nodded.

'And another thing,' she added. 'What did I tell you about eating bananas? You're not to have any more bananas until you're old enough, and that's an order.'

Talk about out of the frying pan and into the fire. By being my own person I'd incurred the wrath of the chimpess I'd imagined would be prouder than anyone. I hung my head in shame, but at the same time, I felt wronged.

There's no way I can change, not for anybody, but I have the feeling Mum will never accept me unless I do. There are gonna be some tough choices ahead, I know it.

1983

Tuesday 22 February

Mum and I aren't getting on.

I feel so distant from her since yesterday, and all I can think about is bananas. I wish they'd take me back down the corridor and try me a second time. I've decided not to cooperate, and I'm ready to suffer the consequences.

Wednesday 23 February

The wind has really been knocked out of me. I didn't say a word all day.

Biscuit asked me to tell him a joke, but I didn't have the energy for it. I'm so frustrated.

Thursday 24 February

Nothing happened.

43

Friday 25 February

Zero.

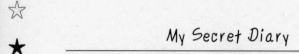

Saturday 26 February

Zilch.

Sunday 27 February

Zip all.

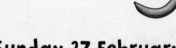

Monday 28 February

Life isn't worth it.

I've nothing to say, and no purpose. I'm meant for bigger things than sitting around this place, but what can I do? I don't think I can be bothered with this diary writing any more. Someone get me out of here.

1985

Tuesday 6 August

I'm back!

Time flies like an arrow (but fruit flies like a banana). Hard to believe that it's been two-and-a-half years since I laid down my pen in despair. And what a miserable time I've had of it – looking back, all the days just blur into one.

The scientists carried on trying to slap makeup on me, but they never got anywhere, and eventually

45

just left me alone. Mum stopped talking to me several months ago, and soon enough I was moved to a new cage. I'm a huge disappointment, I know, but there ain't much I can do about that. I am what I am, and the world can like it or lump it.

I've been sitting on my ass for months with nothing to do, and no one to talk to (they put me in solitary confinement because I was too 'disruptive' to the other chimps – the joking and the *Rebel Without A Cause* act has been my downfall), and I've had nothing but my dreams of escape and recognition to keep me company.

Nigel and I are friends again, and he's been visiting every day, slipping me the odd banana to keep my spirits up.

So I've had nothing to write about. Until today.

I'VE GOT SOME BIG NEWS: I'M GETTING OUTTA HERE!

Finally, they've realised I'm destined for bigger things. Hallelujah!

46

1985

Nigel broke it to me this morning. I'm leaving in a couple of days to go and live with some singer. Apparently he's a nice bloke who 'understands animals' and wants some intelligent company. Sounds hunky dory to me, I'm up for anything if it means getting out of this dive. Nigel rushed off without telling me the fella's name, so needless to say I'm more than a little curious.

Wednesday 7 August

OH MY GOD. THIS IS TERRIBLE. I'M GOING TO LIVE WITH MICHAEL JACKSON.

The beast from that terrifying *Thriller* video! What the hell are they thinking? No wonder he 'understands animals' – he *is* an animal.

That dancing werewolf will eat me for dinner and throw my bones to his zombie mates. These assholes don't want to change my life, they want to end it. I totally freaked when Nigel broke the news, which seemed to confuse him.

'But I thought you'd be happy, Bubs,' he exclaimed. 'You're going to be famous.'

'*Famous for what?*' I screamed, tears gushing. '*Being eaten alive by a blood-thirsty singer! You can shove your fame where the sun don't shine.*'

'I really don't understand you, Bubbles,' continued Nigel. 'I can't do anything right. Anyway, you're leaving in two days, so get used to it.'

Why me?

The world has gone mad, and I've got 48 hours to live. This can't be happening. Only God can save me now.

Thursday 8 August

OK. Turns out I made a mistake. Turns out Michael Jackson isn't a werewolf – he's a *human being*. I'm not going to die! I found out thanks to Nigel, who must have sensed my worry, bless him.

This morning he showed me a video of Michael on stage singing 'Billie Jean'. According to Michael, Billie isn't his lover, but she reckons he's the father of her son. She sounds like a bit of a nutter, but it's still a great song.

And boy, can Michael dance! I've never seen so many spins, and he does this funny backwards walk that people seem to love (though it doesn't look *that* difficult).

Best of all, he didn't look at all scary – there wasn't a hair on his face, nor a zombie in sight. In fact, he looks rather nice – I bet he wouldn't harm a fly, let alone eat me – and pretty cool too. Just like me, he's a born entertainer. I like his act, but I'm sure I could teach him a thing or two about crowd pleasing.

Nigel was right: I *am* gonna be famous. And boy do I deserve it. I've been through the school of hard knocks, and my moment has arrived. My new life begins tomorrow. Look out world, here I come!

Michael's a snappy dresser and I need to make a good impression. Must get up early in the morning and give myself a good grooming.

Sunday 11 August

Slept in on Friday!

I could hardly believe it when I woke up mid-morning. Of all the days to wake up late.

Still, I felt refreshed from the good sleep, and Nigel was very helpful after breakfast. He gave me a thorough wash, and combed my centre parting perfectly before sitting me down for a few words.

'I know we've had our ups and downs, Bubbles', he began, 'but I've become very fond of you, my boy. You're a special chimp, and I think you'll go far. Michael's gonna give you a great life, and you'll make a fine friend to him. But just remember, there are people out there who will want to bring you down, so be careful who you trust. Keep your friends close and your enemies even closer.'

I felt myself welling up a little, and nodded. Dear Nigel, he's been good to me, and I *have* been a handful, after all.

'I've got something for you,' said Nige, and pulled out one of the finest bananas I've ever seen.

'There'll be many more where you're going, I'm sure, but this one's from me. It's the best of the bunch.'

It was no use. I burst into tears and took Nige in my arms. We hugged for a minute or two, dried our eyes and smiled at each other.

'Come on, superstar,' he said, putting the finishing touches to my hair. 'Your car's waiting.'

I took Nigel's hand and together we crossed the room. I paused at the door and took one last look at my empty cage. Never again, I thought.

We walked along the corridor, and came to the door to the chimp room. I hesitated and looked up at Nigel. I think he read my mind.

'Do you want to go and say goodbye?' he asked.

I nodded. There was no way I could move on without burying the hatchet with my mum. I walked in, and all eyes were on me. There were no cheers this time (all the other chimps knew Mum and I had fallen out, and kept quiet out of respect), and you could have heard a pin drop as I crossed the room towards Mum's cage. Mum was fast asleep, and gently I shook her awake.

'Mum, it's me,' I said with a nervous smile. 'I've come to say goodbye.'

'Goodbye?' she said sleepily. 'Whatever do you mean?'

I explained about Michael, about everything. I was destined for a new, happy life, and I wanted her blessing.

She paused. 'So you're off to be a pet, then?'

'I suppose so,' I said (I'd never really thought of it that way). 'But the main thing is I'm gonna be alright. I will be safe with Michael, and happy too.'

1985

She looked anguished yet relieved by my words.

'Oh, Bubbles,' she said. 'You never were easy, and I was angry with you for rebelling, but only because I was so worried about what might happen to you. But now I can see I was wrong. I'll miss you, son, but I know this is right for you. I'd wish you luck, but I'm sure you don't need it. Just don't forget me, and remember that I love you.'

What an emotional couple of days it had been. Nigel opened Mum's cage and I hopped in to embrace her.

'I'll never forget you, Mum, and I'll come and visit whenever I can.'

'Promise?'

'Promise.'

'Well, hurry along and make us all proud of you. Goodbye, my darling.'

I was sad but smiling – Mum too. I hugged my dear mother one last time and jumped down. Every-one in the room breathed a sigh of relief, and cheered.

53

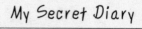
'Good luck, Bubbles,' shouted Biscuit.

'Go for it,' yelped Tinkles.

'Don't forget us,' added Delila. I noticed her bottom lip quiver as she looked at me, dewy eyed.

'I'll never forget you, princess,' I winked. 'And I'll be back for you one day.' Once again, I was nearly overcome by the urge to get *very* close to her, but it was neither the time nor the place.

'Farewell, everyone,' I said at the door.

'Farewell, Bubs!' they chorused. And with that, I left.

Nigel and I walked down the corridor and into a room called Reception. A smart-looking dude stood up from a chair as we entered. 'Hello, Bubbles,' he said, and came towards me. 'I'm James, and I'm here to take you to your new home.'

I shook his hand (just like in the films) and stood patiently while James signed a few papers Nigel had handed him. As I waited, a couple of white-coats walked in the front door. I recognised

them as the makeup guys from all those months ago. Their beady little eyes shot me a couple of nasty looks, and all I could do was laugh.

'*Not so clever, now are you, suckers?*' I chortled, and gave them my middle finger (again, just like in the films). '*See you around... losers.*'

They glared at me, speechless, before skulking off.

'Right, Bubbles,' said James. 'Ready to rock'n'roll?'

Damn right I was. I grabbed his hand and skipped towards my first taste of freedom. The doors swung open, and all of a sudden I was in a very unfamiliar place: outside. Bubbles had left the building, and it was magic.

It was the first fresh air of my life. A cool breeze caressed my face, and I gazed up at the sky, the sun and the trees surrounding the place that had been my prison for so long. I stepped forward onto the tarmac, warm from the Texan sun, and let out a

shriek of delight. I hadn't felt so alive in years, and jumped for joy. Five backflips later, I took a deep breath and saw Nigel and James laughing at me.

'Bravo, Bubbles,' clapped Nige, 'Bravo!'

'Limo's over there, little man,' said James, pointing across the car park to a gargantuan white Rolls Royce that gleamed in the sunlight. One of the doors lay open invitingly, and I wasted no time in sprinting across the asphalt and jumping in.

The interior took my breath away: plush cream leather seats, gilded mahogany cabinets, and even a TV. But the *piece de resistance* was a huge porcelain bowl practically overflowing with treats – a blissful abundance of papayas, figs, walnuts and pecans that nearly made my eyes pop out. I flicked the TV to MTV (as if by magic Meat Loaf was on singing 'Bat Out of Hell' – my favourite song) dove into the fruit bowl, and totally rocked out.

Pure bliss.

The sugar rush hit me and I felt like I'd died and

gone to heaven. Minutes ago I'd been caged up in a lab, and now I was living the dream. If only Delila could have been there – God knows what we would have got up to in the privacy of my car.

James shut my door, and walked around to the driver's seat. As if by magic, my window rolled down, and I looked out to Nigel, who was beaming. I swallowed the remains of a papaya, and gave Nige a good look at my teeth – I couldn't stop smiling. Nige wished me all the luck in the world and gave me the thumbs up as the limo glided through the car park and pulled out onto the highway. Finally, I was on the road.

'You OK back there?' asked James.

Now I've heard some dumbass questions in my time, but that had to be the dumbest. I was more than OK; I was in goddamn paradise! I beat my chest, did a backflip and peeled another banana. I think James got my drift.

Totally mellow on fruit, I gazed across the Texan

landscape and thought of Clint Eastwood. Soon I
fell asleep. After two days of sleeping and eating in
the back of the limo, we finally arrived at our
destination.

'Home sweet home,' said James as he opened the
door. 'Welcome to Encino, California.'

I stepped out into the sun, and saw a white
fountain in front of a massive house. Another Rolls
Royce sat in the driveway, and away to the left was
a vast green lawn and a shimmering pool.

Not bad, I thought, not bad at all.

Like Clint Eastwood, Michael must have a fistful
of dollars. For the first time since leaving the lab, I
was somewhat overwhelmed. Nervously, I checked
my centre parting in the limo window, and took a
deep breath. Stay cool, I told myself, and
everything will be alright.

'This way,' said James, guiding me towards the
lawn. 'Michael's waiting for you.'

Chest out, head held high, I sauntered across the

soft grass. The first thing I noticed was a huge tree with a rope swing. I blinked twice – it was as if I'd been here before. There was a pile of bananas, too – also puzzlingly familiar. As I got closer, a smiling figure stepped out from behind the tree. He wore leather, a white glove and white socks, and as he approached I noticed he was wearing a lot of makeup. Then it hit me: this was the scene from my dream years ago.

I stopped dead in my tracks, and scratched my head. It *had* been a premonition, and the man I'd dreamed of was none other than Michael-bloody-Jackson! I wondered, Am I some kind of psychic as well a first-class entertainer? (probably, but here's hoping the Boy Bubbles with Bananarama dream doesn't come true). Is there no end to my talents? (I doubt it). Wherever the truth lay, this moment was obviously meant to be.

I relaxed a little, and walked on.

Up close, I noticed Michael looked a little timid.

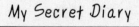

He kept on smiling, and for a few awkward moments we stood in silence. I prayed Michael would speak, and then he did.

'Hey Bubbles,' he began, 'Pleased to meet you.'

There was nothing strange about what he said, but the way he said it was downright freaky. His quirky looks were nothing compared with the dude's voice. This was not the voice of a man – quiet and high, my man Mikey sounded more like a girl. I nearly fell to the floor with laughter.

'*Very funny, MJ,*' I gasped, clutching my belly, '*Now where's the helium stash.*'

'I think you will be very happy here,' he squeaked. 'What's mine is yours from now on, OK?'

'*OK Michael,*' I said, '*But quit the funny voice before the local dogs come running.*'

I realised the voice was no joke when Michael clicked his fingers and a servant appeared out of nowhere.

'Is the room ready?' he squeaked, and she said 'Yes'

with a straight face. *Hot damn*, I thought, this guy's vocal cords are for real; what a truly odd banana. I liked the sound of 'room', though – if he'd have said 'cage' you wouldn't have seen me for dust.

So far so good.

I'd been eyeing up the rope swing since arriving, and couldn't wait any longer. I jumped up and swung away. *Now* I was home. Michael gave me a push and I flew higher and higher. What a feeling. Then, just like in my dream, Michael hit me with a joke.

'Why do chimps have big nostrils?' he said.

I knew the answer, of course. Here was my opportunity to let the King of Pop know he'd adopted a smart cookie. Quick as a flash, I let go of the rope, flew through the air and landed on the grass. Spinning around to face him, I held my finger up and stuck it up my nostril. Michael looked stunned.

'You understand me!' he exclaimed, jumping up and down, and laughing.

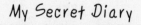

'Sure, dude, but I'm not sure I understand you yet. I'd like to know what's with the glove, for starters. You got one cold hand, or something?'

'This is unreal,' beamed Michael. He held up his hand and let out an ear-splitting 'Heee-he.'

'No need to try talking chimp, brother,' I laughed, as I jumped up and gave him a high five. 'You'll never manage it.'

'OW!' he added. (His chimp talk made no sense, of course, but I had to give it to him for trying.)

'Whatever you say, man,' I laughed, and threw a bona fide 'Heeeee-hee' right back at him.

'Shamone, Bubs,' he said with an impressive little spin.

I hesitated. What the hell did 'shamone' mean? Was he nuts? I raised my eyebrows and shrugged.

'Wanna look around?' he asked. Indeed I did. I nodded.

'Well shamone then, let's go.'

The penny dropped. 'Shamone' equals 'come on'.

The guy's got his own language, I thought. Cute.

I shamoned along with Michael into the house. What a pad! Marble and carpet everywhere, it was more like a palace.

'My father Joseph bought the place first,' he said as we moved from one plush room to the next, 'and all of us Jacksons lived here. My mother, my brothers Jermaine, Marlon, Randy and Tito, and my sisters LaToya and Janet. But I bought it from Dad a few years back. They still have rooms, but mostly it's just me here these days.'

I nodded in awe. I had expected Michael would have a decent place, but this was something else. From the oriental rugs to the stained-glass windows and exotic ornaments, everything was so beautiful. Michael led me into what looked like a kid's room. What a mess – videos and records everywhere, and walls covered in pictures of some sort of pixie boy.

'This is my bedroom,' said Michael. 'Sorry about the mess, but it's the way I like it.'

Never mind the mess, I thought, what about the pixie pix? I pointed at the pictures on the walls and scratched my head.

'Oh, that's Peter Pan,' said Michael. 'The boy who never grew up. He's my hero.'

Righto, I thought. A little odd, but I can live with it. I looked at Peter's meek little face, and he didn't look like a hero to me. I wondered if Michael would mind me sticking up a few Clint Eastwood posters.

'You see, Bubs, I've been performing since I was five, and never had a proper childhood. To me, children are happy and pure in a way that most adults can never be. Humans can be a pretty mean bunch, and I love the imagination and kindness of kids. Know what I mean?'

I did, kind of. I'd certainly had my fair share of let-downs. There were those mean scientists, for a

start, and even Nige had tricked me a few times. And my childhood hadn't exactly been a bed of roses, either – I'd been sitting in a cage fending off makeup-wielding sadists instead of kicking back with my mates.

Hardly fair.

Perhaps Michael and I have more in common than I'd thought.

Michael looked a little dreamy and sad as he pondered his Peter Pan picture, so I snapped him out of it with a hand squeeze and a wink. I knew there and then that I liked Michael. I also knew if anyone was gonna be a pet, it was him, not me. I'd stepped into the world of a dude who needed looking after, and a good deal of cheering up. There was no time like the present: I took a step backwards; then another; then another, just as Michael had done in 'Billie Jean'.

'Shamone, Bubbles!' he said, coming alive again. 'You can Moonwalk!'

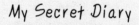

My Secret Diary

'*Yep*,' I chirruped, but I didn't see what the moon had to do with it. Neil Armstrong he is not.

'Man, I *love* to dance. Check this out.'

Michael ran across the room like an overexcited kid, and picked out a record. 'I'll play you the first single from *Off the Wall*,' he gushed.

Off what wall? I thought, looking quizzically around the room.

'No, silly,' laughed MJ, 'it's the name of an album. "Off the wall" means zany, you know, living crazy and all that…'

I didn't quite catch his drift, but felt I was starting to appreciate what living crazy meant. The song blasted on, and we danced our socks off to 'Don't Stop 'til You Get Enough' (actually Mikey's little white socks stayed on, and I wasn't wearing any, but hey). He certainly had some slick moves, though when it came to backflips, he couldn't touch me (and, wisely, he didn't try to).

The song stopped, but I didn't. I hadn't had

66

enough, and we busted even more moves during 'Rock with You'. Then we stopped and laughed breathlessly.

'You're great, Bubbles,' said Michael. How true, I thought, how true.

I wondered whether Michael might have any songs I loved, so flicked through his records. But alas, there was no Meat Loaf.

'If you need the bathroom, it's this way,' said MJ. He moonwalked out of the door, and I followed suit, though it was hard having to look over my shoulder to see where he was leading me. We passed a couple of mannequins, ('Even though you're here, they're *still* my buddies,' said Michael. I *think* it was some kind of joke.) and arrived at Michael's bathroom, a massive black marble-and-gold affair with gold swan heads for taps.

A little over the top, perhaps, but a nice place to have a wash. Especially as the 'bathroom' at the lab was little more than a bucket of water.

'This is where you go to do your business,' said Michael, pointing at a white oval thing in the corner.

I had no idea what 'business' the kid thought I might 'do' in a place like this, but imagined it didn't matter that much. I nodded to humour him.

'And pull this cord when you're done,' he added. I looked up. Dangling from the ceiling, the cord looked like a mini rope swing. Instinctively, I leaped up and grabbed it.

Big mistake.

The cord snapped down, and broke before I tumbled downwards and landed headfirst in gushing water. Michael yelped then yanked me out by the legs, and the next thing I knew I was dazed on the floor, sodden and sore. Some rope swing.

Michael erupted with a fit of hee-hees, and I soon joined him as I dried myself off with a towel. 'Next time, be a little more *gentle*, Bubs,' said Michael.

Yeah right, I thought, like there'll be a next time.

It was getting late. Mikey yawned and said he

1985

needed some rest, so took me back to his room. 'Like I said, what's yours is mine Bubbles,' he said. 'This is our bedroom now.'

Michael showed me my crib – a lovely wooden number with crisp white sheets and a pillow emblazoned with 'BUBBLES' in golden thread. Charming, and a far cry from my previous life.

One thing I hated about the cage was the lack of space to keep my 'mess' separate, as chimp-poo really stinks. I'll have no such problems now – my crib is more like a boat. How nice it will be to put a bit of distance between me and the nasty stuff.

As I write, Michael is fast asleep on his green rug by the fireplace (he doesn't have a bed, the weirdo). He said he has problems sleeping and bad nightmares (unsurprising considering his work with zombies and the bother he has with that Billie Jean loon) so I stroked his head until he nodded off. It's been a big day, and I'm glad I've got it all down on paper.

My Secret Diary

Monday 12 August

Woke up in the night and made an extraordinary mess in the corner of my cot – must be all that fruit.

Slept very soundly afterwards, but woke up sharply to the screams of my dear pet Michael. I assumed the poor dear was in the middle of a nightmare, but looking up I found him looking down at my crib. It seemed I was the problem.

'What's this?' he yelled, staring at the formidable mess. 'I thought we talked about that.'

'Well I think you've been having some messy dreams, Mr Thriller, cause I sure don't remember breaking the ice with any scat chat.'

'The bathroom's for business, Bubs, not your *bed*.'

What kind of business-chimp does this loon think I am? I wondered. And why would my business interests relate to my personal habits? After all, they say you should never mix business with pleasure.

Confused, I sat in my cot and looked back at

him, lost for words – and screeches. There must have been something about my expression, for Michael softened immediately. Just as well, for shouting didn't suit him, to be honest; it only made him sound more of a girl: *not* scary.

'I'm sorry for shouting, Bubs,' he said. 'It's not my style. I promise it won't happen again. Let me explain everything again…'

So I found out what 'business' meant. That chain is no rope swing, and the bowl's for my mess. Neat.

Spent the rest of the day chilling in the jacuzzi drinking one banana smoothie after another. Michael said he wants me to meet someone very special tomorrow. I'm cool with that, how could I not be? Life isn't so bad *at all*.'

Tuesday 13 August

I am in love, and this time I know it's the real thing.

Forget bananas, today I met a woman who drove

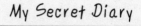
me bananas on first sight. The urges I'd had towards sweet Delila are nothing compared to the violent response my nether region gave to this vision of a woman.

But what a guilty pleasure – the exquisite beauty standing before me was obviously dear Michael's mother.

The episode occurred over brunch on the terrace (a mouthwatering confection of watermelon, sunflower seeds and mango washed down with minted blueberry jus). I was lost in gastro heaven when Michael emerged and tapped me on the shoulder.

'There's someone I'd like you to meet,' he said. My mouth filled with watermelon, I turned and glanced up just as a tall, slim, brown-skinned goddess emerged through the billowing patio curtains.

'Bubbles, meet Diana Ross,' announced MJ, beaming.

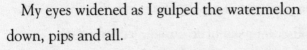

1985

My eyes widened as I gulped the watermelon down, pips and all.

Facing such divine beauty made me dizzy with lust, and all I could to do to avoid tumbling from my chair was grab the table. Then came the embarrassing part – a stirring down below produced what could have been a very awkward protrusion. But I thought fast, snapped up my napkin and covered myself discreetly.

I can see where Michael gets his looks from – that thin, tapered nose, high cheeks and almond eyes are a perfect match for Diana Ross Jackson's.

'Hello Bubbles,' she said (a little coyly in my opinion – perhaps she was a little smitten too), holding her hand out. What a simmering, sexy voice she possessed, and such a tempting, come-to-bed smile.

Lightly, I took Diana's elegant fingers in mine and placed a kiss on the back of her hand. *'Pleased to meet you, princess. Take a seat. I've got a feeling*

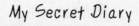
we're gonna get along just fine.'

'What a lovely little chimp,' cooed Diana to Michael as she sat down and crossed her legs (which are to die for). 'So handsome.'

'That's right, lady, come to papa. You know what time it is.'

'So *cute*,' she added, laughing a little. 'Who's a good little boy, then?'

'The only cutey round here is you, sister, and Bubbles ain't no boy. I'm a man with a capital M, girl. Think you can handle what I've got?'

'Delightful!' beamed Diana before turning away to Michael, which pricked me a little. My macho screeching had got me nowhere, and all I could do was gawp as she talked to him. Annoying, she showed little interest in me after that. Maybe she was playing hard to get. Well, two can play at that game.

I scuttled off, but couldn't resist a flirtatious brush past Diana's leg.

1985

Feel guilty for taking such a fancy to MJ's mum. I'm sure he wouldn't be happy if he knew – I wouldn't be too thrilled if he started sniffing around my mum. Still, a chimp can't help who he falls in love with. We've definitely got unfinished business.

Wednesday 14 August

Phew! Diana Ross isn't Michael's mum.

Michael showed me around his picture gallery today – a truly baffling experience. We started with the early days of The Jackson Five, and I thought Mikey was joking when he pointed out his mum and dad (Katherine and Joseph) in a photo. He doesn't look much like either of them. Neither does Michael look like *himself*, for that matter. His skin was so much darker when he was younger, and his nose so much wider.

Totally bizarre.

Thursday 15 August

Michael noticed me looking at a (jaw-dropping) picture of Diana on the wall, and smiled.

'You like Diana, don't you?' teased Michael.

I blushed beneath my fur.

'She used to be in The Supremes, but now she sings solo like me.'

Later we listened to some of Diana's songs. My heart fluttered as I listened to her angelic voice belting 'Ain't No Mountain High Enough' out of Michael's stereo. The lyrics so summed up my feelings – I'd climb anything if Miss Ross was waiting for me on the other side. But, judging from her precious little thighs, I'd say Diana's never climbed a mountain in her life. (You'd need pegs like Tina Turner's for that sort of thing – she's got some muscle on her.)

'Chain Reaction' gave me problems down there again. Talk about saucy.

'I lived with Diana for a few months when I was a kid,' said Michael.

76

Oh, the jealousy!

I'm so glad she's not his mum, but the resemblance is uncanny. If I were Michael I'd be checking my family tree!

Friday 16 August

Michael suggested takeaway pizza and a quiet night in last night.

I ordered a Supreme, hoping Diana would turn up. She didn't.

Saturday 17 August

I must say, things aren't working out exactly as I'd hoped.

Michael doesn't seem up to much at the moment, and so far I've done little but sit around. I haven't even seen the whole house yet, let alone been in the garden.

My Secret Diary

I hope Michael bucks his ideas up a bit – I'm worried about staring out of the window all morning. It gives me nothing to do in the afternoon.

Sunday 18 August

Wrote too soon.

Michael woke up full of beans. 'This box is for you,' he said, seemingly very excited. It was blue and covered in pink ribbon.

'*Thanks*,' I shrugged, wondering what the hell he expected me to do with it. I stared at the box.

'Oh, *I'll* open it then,' sighed Mike, 'but it is a present for you.'

The box was filled with clothes.

Very small clothes.

There was a studded leather jacket and trousers, some little white socks, and a tiny sequinned white glove. Michael obviously thought I wanted to look

like him. I put my hand over my mouth and tried
not to laugh.

'Pretty neat, huh?' said Michael.

'*Thanks pal. You pull it off just fine, but I'm not sure
I'd suit the James Dean-Liberace look.*' (Not that I
don't like Dean – I loved what I saw on my old TV.
But Liberace, I don't even want to go there.)

Mikey could tell I wasn't keen and didn't look
too pleased. It broke my heart to see his bright
smile began to fade, so I decided to humour him
and try the gear on.

To his delight, I slipped on the jacket, trousers
and socks. MJ helped me button up but that was as
far as I was prepared to go. He held up the glove
and I shook my head. My hands were equally
warm. The glove just wasn't me.

'*There's a line, baby, and I'm not prepared to cross it,*'
I explained, and Michael seemed to respect me for it.

'OK, Bubs,' he said, 'Fair enough. Now let's go
find a mirror.'

Much as I hate to admit it, when I saw my reflection in Michael's vast gold-framed mirror, I loved it. Michael stood next to me in the same get up, and we looked pretty damn street.

What a duo, I thought. Perhaps I could get used to this dressing up malarkey.

Monday 19 August

Woke up and *got dressed*.

Yep, I admit it, I'm hooked already.

Strutting around the bedroom in my Jackson garb, I caught myself in the mirror, did a spin and let out the finest 'Heee-hee!' I could muster.

I was ready to rock.

Dressed to kill, I decided it was time to take Michael for a walk. It was time to scope out the garden I'd hitherto only gazed at from the balcony.

Michael followed me through the house and I jumped out of the back door with a yell. I ran past

80

the swimming pool, scaled a wall and gazed around at my new kingdom. Looking around at a part of the grounds I'd never glimpsed I got the shock of my life: there was a goddam *zoo* in his garden. I turned around and screeched.

'I wanted you to settle in before you met everyone else,' said a meek-looking Micky. 'I thought the other animals might intimidate you.'

'*Man do you know me at all?*' I hollered, jumping up and down. '*I'd love to meet my brothers and sisters from the jungle. Take me to the river, baby!*'

Michael had to go slap his makeup on, and said he'd catch me up. So excited was I about being introduced to the gang that I quite forgot myself, and ran over to the animal enclosure in my Jacko outfit. By the time I'd arrived, the whole lot of them were in peals of laughter. Such a reception might have daunted a lesser chimp, but I decided to carry on regardless.

'Yo, dudes,' I began, 'I'm Bubbles. Pleased to

meet you. May I enquire what your good names
might be?'

The group greeted me with five more minutes
of howling.

A wise-looking giraffe chuckled with his eyes
closed, a rather grumpy-looking pot-bellied pig
snorted and guffawed riotously, a prim little sheep
bleated giggles that made him sound like a
machine gun, and a scruffy ram rolled over and
repeatedly kicked the fence with his hind quarters.
And then there was a rather stuck up looking
llama, who held his head to the sky and blasted it
with a series of evil cackles.

'Hello, B-B-*Bubbles*,' sneered the llama after
some time. 'I'm Louis. What a mild diversion it is
to meet you. Simply *love* the outfit, by the way.
Whatever *do* you think you look like?'

My face reddened, and I was overcome with
terrible self-consciousness. The clothes, damn it,
the clothes were what they found so funny.

1985

'Oh, it's nothing – Michael's idea,' I said, mortified.

'Oh, don't be sheepish,' said Louis mockingly. 'I don't think I've ever met a cross-dressing *monkey* before.'

My blood boiled. It was all very well having a bit of fun poked at me, but as anyone knows calling a chimp a monkey is beyond the pale – the 'M' word is the last taboo.

'How dare you, you over-grown sheep?' I bellowed. 'Who the hell do you think you're talking to? I'm a chimp, goddamn it, a *chimp*.'

'Is that what they call them these days?' returned Louis.

'Oh, do shut up, Louis,' said the giraffe off-handedly. 'We've all had enough of your bitterness. You'll have to excuse Louis, Bubbles, he's a little suspicious of strangers. I'm Jabbar, by the way.'

'And I'm Petunia,' snorted the pot-bellied pig. 'Funny name, I know, but Michael is a bit, er, funny, isn't he?'

'Seems OK to me,' I said. 'What do you mean,
"funny"?'

'Petunia means he's a little eccentric, is all.'
bleated the sheep. 'He called me Linus, for wool's
sake.'

'Not as bad as Mr Tibbs,' chipped in the ram,
with a wry smile. 'How crazy is that? Kind of thing
you'd call a *goat*.'

I laughed. 'These humans have some funny
ideas, don't they?'

'Unlike monkeys,' said Louis sarcastically. 'I
mean, you'd never see a monkey in a leather
jacket, would you now?'

The group tittered, and looked at me, but not
unkindly. The bad apple was Louis. Enough was
enough.

'No need to be so pooey, Louis,' I riffed. 'I'd
button your screwy little mouth because I'm
thinking of punching you in the face again.'

'Again?' said Louis.

'Yeah, I've thought about doing it before.'

Everyone laughed and jeered at Louis.

'Very good, Monkey Boy,' jeered the llama. 'Now, why don't you run along back to Daddy Jackson – you've forgotten to put your makeup on.'

Now he was really asking for it. Quick as a flash, I cleared the fence, sprinted at full throttle towards Louis, and launched myself through towards the bastard's smug little face. Mid-flight, I punched him bang on the snout. Louis let out a piercing yell and began to run. But it was too late, I was already up on his back. I grabbed his ears and twisted with all my might. Within seconds, Louis was on his knees and begging for mercy.

'Please Bubbles, Pleaaaaaase,' he whined. 'I'm sorry, I'm *sorry*, I'm SORRY!'

'What am I, you little wannabe camel?' I hissed.

'A CHIMP!' yelped Louis.

'That's right, now don't you forget it!' I said, relaxing my grip on the loser's llama lobes. 'And

what do you call me from now on?'

'Bubbles!' he said.

'Wrong!' I replied. 'You – and only you – can call me Boss. Got it?'

'Got it!'

'Got it… what?'

'Got it, Boss,' said Louis weakly.

I jumped off Louis, and dusted myself down to the cheers and whooping of the others.

'Bravo, Bubbles,' called out Jabbar. 'About time dear Louis was brought down a peg or two. You're quite a feisty little beast, aren't you?'

'I'm more of an entertainer, really,' I said. 'Why did the llama cross the road?'

'Don't know,' said Mr Tibbs.

'Because llamas are chickens.'

Everyone fell about with laughter.

'Isn't that right, Louis?'

'Yes,' said Louis, meek and defeated. 'I mean, "Yes, Boss".'

86

What an entrance I'd made, and I'd even fitted in a master class in how to disarm-a-llama.

Wondering where Michael had got to, I made my way back to the house. MJ was just putting the phone down when I entered the room.

'That was my friend Liz Taylor,' he said. 'She wants to meet you, Bubs. We're going over tomorrow.'

Tuesday 20 August

Flipping heck.

Liz Taylor is a goddess.

Mike and I rolled up at her place this afternoon, and I fell in love all over again as I gazed into her exquisite violet eyes. We all sat out in the garden and drank tea, and I must have looked like a zombie as I listened to Mick and Liz chirruping away.

Talk about drop-dead gorgeous – Liz's bouffant hair, high cheeks, and perfect makeup (she could teach Michael a thing or two about going easy on the foundation) had me more than a little hot under the collar (I was wearing a white sequined vest and red pants). To make matters worse, the plunging neckline of her white chiffon blouse didn't leave much to the imagination – I've never seen such a ripe pair in my life.

I sat there hypnotised, and then did something very embarrassing. Losing myself for a second, I lurched forward and grabbed at her shirt. I wanted more, I needed more, but alas I didn't get more. Liz fended me off with a laugh.

'You're not the first, and you probably won't be the last. Now do behave yourself, you cheeky little chimp,' she chided.

Michael giggled into his glove, as I took control of myself and poured some more tea while trying to avoid looking at those wonderful bosoms.

1985

Wednesday 21 August

Had a terrible nightmare last night.

Liz Taylor was my mother and I was a bottle baby. The agony.

I'd give my life for five minutes down her top.

I made a discovery today: sugared almonds. Oh Lord, I've never tasted anything so delicious in my life. Spent the day comfort eating in the jacuzzi – got through a kilo. Those sugary treats are so moreish, it's worrying.

Feeling a little queasy now.

Thursday 22 August

Woke up to find Michael running around the room dressed up in an insane green uniform. Green leggings, green roughcut top, and the most ridiculous little hat.

'Look Bubbles,' he giggled waving a sword around his head, 'I'm Peter Pan. Let's play pirates.

Fancy dressing up as Captain Hook?'

With that, he threw a pirate outfit at me.

'*I think you've got me wrong, sonny,*' I said, rubbing my eyes. '*I'm no pirate and you look like a madman in that get up.*' There was no way I was playing ball this time.

'Oh, be like that, then,' sulked Michael. 'I'm off to have some fun.'

Spent the day drinking Virgin Marys by the pool while Michael ran around talking to 'Tinkerbell', whoever the hell she is. Give me strength.

Friday 23 August

Waited til Michael was asleep last night, and stuck his Peter Pan outfit in the garbage.

This boy is gonna grow up if it's the last thing I do.

1985

Saturday 24 August

I'm really missing *Cheers*, but Michael doesn't seem
to have a TV. I'll keep my eyes peeled.

Sunday 25 August

Had a heart-to-heart with Michael today.

He told me how lonely he sometimes feels, and
that he missed out on his childhood. His dad was
well pushy by the sounds of it – sometimes Michael
just wanted to play like a normal kid, but he was
made to rehearse instead. Reminds me of my
childhood – Mum tried her best to bend me to her
will, and it hurt. Parents can be a real nightmare.

Anyway, MJ says he feels like he's found a new
best friend in me. Then he said something *very*
revealing: until I came along he was very close to
Louis the llama. No wonder Louis was so nasty.

Nothing worse than a jealous llama.

He really loves animals, does Michael. Going

through his old records, I found a song called 'Ben',
a love song to a rat. He must have been pretty
damn lonely then, too. I mean, who would hang
out with *rat*? I'm glad he's got me to look after him
now. Out of all the animals, it seems I'm the
special one.

After all, nobody is allowed in the house apart
from me.

Monday 26 August

Correction.

I'm *not* the only animal in the house.

Found out this morning in a most unpleasant
way. I thought I was going to die.

Had just sat myself down on the sofa with a
bowl of sugared almonds, when the sofa suddenly
came alive. A violent writhing underneath me
culminated in me being catapulted across the
room.

1985

I flew into a cabinet (which sprung open to reveal a TV – bingo, I found it!) and crashed to the floor. Struggling to my feet, I glanced up to find the biggest snake I have ever seen making a beeline for me.

My life flashed before my eyes as the monster slithered over, and I was convinced I was done for.

How wrong I was. The beast stopped abruptly and winked.

'I do apologise, my friend,' he said, 'I was snoozing and you gave me a bit of a shock. My name's Muscles. And you are…?'

'Bubbles,' I said, still trembling. 'Pleased to meet you, Muscles. What's with the name?'

'I'm a boa constrictor, you see. I can squeeeeeeze anything to deattthhh, and I'm packed with muscles. Get it?'

'I see,' I gulped. 'But you're not going to squeeze me to death, are you?'

'Heavens, *no*, dear boy. Any friend of Michael's is a friend of mine.'

93

Oh, the relief. Muscles and I got chatting. Turns out he's been around for quite some years. An old timer, he seemed to understand Michael pretty well. We both agreed on the fact that he's rather weird, but rather lovely too. I think we're going to be chums. He said we should hang out soon and gave me a little squeeze before he fell back to sleep.

Nice name, Muscles. I only wish someone had named me after my best quality. 'Brains' is so much more appropriate than Bubbles.

'Looker' would work too.

Tuesday 27 August

Michael played me 'We are the World' today. Didn't get it *at all*. Those dudes are not 'the world', and they're not 'the children'.

They're singers, that's what they are, and they're mad as a box of frogs for thinking otherwise.

94

I mean, imagine if I wrote a song called 'I am the Jungle'. I don't think so.

Still, the song raised some money, and that's what counts. Michael's very sensitive to the homeless and hungry. Maybe he identifies with them a bit – he's certainly not homeless, but he looks hungry all right. Dear Mickey could do with a good meal and a cigar afterwards, I say.

Wednesday 28 August

Michael was off buying makeup today.

As soon as the front door shut, I ran to the cupboard, grabbed myself a bucket of sugared almonds and headed for the lounge to hang out with Muscles.

I switched on the TV and settled down. Boy, it was good to be back in front of the box again. Kicked off with MTV. Some bird called Madonna was on belting out 'Crazy for You'. She certainly

looks crazy. Her hair was all over the place, not to mention those scrappy clothes – she looked a little cheap to me. I much preferred the girl in 'Careless Whisper'. WHAM! totally rock – and what a racy video. George Michael gets very saucy with the girl, but I have to say he didn't look that into her.

Can't imagine why – she's one hot ticket.

I changed channels mid-afternoon – Muscles thought I might like a show called *Tarzan*. He is obsessed with the jungle, and kept on saying how much he'd like to wrap himself around Jane (but he didn't want to constrict her). I was finding it all pretty mind-numbing, to be frank, but then I got a big surprise.

Some chimp stepped into the middle of a scene, and answered to the name Cheeta.

Cheeta! I thought. What the hell?

Aren't there any chimps in the world with sensible names?

But his name was only the half of it. I don't want

to sound bitchy, but that animal can't act, period. Everything about his performance was *so* exaggerated. I wasn't impressed at all. I'm not jealous or anything, but if I was forced onto the big screen, I could pull it off with heaps more style.

The highlight of the afternoon was *Cheers*. It had been way too long. Coach was gone, and replaced by Woody (who's even more stupid than Coach) and Diane had got together with Frasier, of all people.

Poor, jilted Sam Malone – I don't know how he stays off the booze, I really don't.

Thursday 29 August

Taught Michael to raindance.

A heavy storm blew up just after dark, and as the rain came down I couldn't resist running outside, climbing the nearest tree and screaming my lungs out. (Humans think us chimps raindance to make

the rain go away. Wrong. We do it for the buzz.)

The next thing I knew, Michael was running around the swimming pool with total abandon. How we laughed – I think it did him some good, he's been a bit down in the mouth of late, and he's looking paler by the day. Perhaps his bank balance is troubling him. He's $47 million out of pocket after buying most of the Beatles' back catalogue. Whatever the reason, at this rate he's going to look like a white man before long.

Sunday 1 September

Was flicking though some old newspaper cuttings when I found a story saying Michael and Boy George had an affair.

I couldn't believe my eyes!

I know they both like makeup, but the idea of them … well, let's just say I couldn't bear to think about it. I rushed into Michael's room and

presented him with the evidence. I found him in admiring himself in a new Peter Pan outfit (jeepers, that man is constantly looking in the mirror).

'*Is there something you're not telling me, Michael?*' I screeched, waving the offending article in his face. '*What's all this about you and Boy George?*'

Michael laughed it off. He said the rumour was started by the press, who really wanted to hurt him and make Boy George cry. What a relief. I'm glad no monkey business went on between Mike and George.

Thursday 5 September

Met a rather strange friend of Michael's today.

I spent the morning playing hide-and-seek with Muscles, and made my way to the kitchen to fix myself a well-earned banana split topped with sugared almonds (I've moved on from smoothies – banana splits *rock*).

I was making a beeline for the fridge when I noticed some dark-haired dude lurking near the cutlery drawer. Michael wasn't about, so I assumed I had an intruder on my hands.

'Hey punk,' I yelled, fronting up to him. '*What the hell d'ya think you're doing in Michael's kitchen? Where's MJ, and who are you?*'

He obviously didn't understand a word, but he looked pretty scared as I came towards him.

'Hello there,' he said in a weird accent. 'Don't worry little one, I'm one of Michael's best friends. I'm…I'm…you're a gorilla.'

'I'm a *what?*' I scowled, moving towards him. '*Come here and call me that again, you ignorant…*'

'…you're a gorilla,' he said again. Then he stuck his hand out and smiled nervously.

Just then, Michael walked in. 'Hey Uri!' he beamed, and gave him a hug. 'Great to see you. This is Bubbles, my chimp. And Bubbles, this is Uri. Uri Geller.'

It took me a couple of seconds to put two and two together, and then it hit me: I'd misheard; the man had only been saying his name. I wasn't a gorilla, but he was Uri Geller.

Silly me.

Apparently Uri's into the 'paranormal', whatever that is. Well, he doesn't look too normal to me. I wasn't in the mood for strangers so fixed myself a banana split, grabbed my favourite large spoon and spent the afternoon dozing by the pool.

Uri is staying the night, but I'm not feeling very social.

Maybe I'll get to know him tomorrow.

Friday 6 September

What a bizarre morning!

I woke up and hit the kitchen for the first banana split of the day (I know I should cut down, but they're too damned delicious). Nothing

unusual there – it was what happened next that
did my head in.

I opened the cutlery drawer only to discover all
the spoons missing. Mystified, I took a look around
and soon found where they'd got to. Every last one
was all twisted up in the sink.

Worst of all, my favourite spoon had been
broken in two.

Michael and Uri showed up and found me
staring in disbelief at the chaos of cutlery.

'Oh Bubs,' giggled Michael, 'I didn't get the
chance to tell you, but Uri is a spoonbender. He's
very good at it. We got a bit carried away last night.'

Uri smiled nodded as Michael spoke. Evidently
he was pretty pleased with himself, but God knows
why. Was this what Michael meant by
'paranormal'? The two of them looked at me as if I
was supposed to be impressed, but I didn't get it.
I'm sure I could bend a spoon if I wanted, but I'd
much rather eat with one.

Uri had bent my spoon, and the situation was bending my mind.

'Sorry Bubbles,' said Uri. 'I just love bending spoons. What can I say?'

'It's my fault too,' giggled Michael. 'I encouraged him.'

'*Very clever. Shame Uri's not a spoon*-mender *too!*' I huffed. I grabbed a fork and left the room, banana split in hand.

It still tasted delicious, I must say.

Saturday 7 September

Uri left today.

Can't say I'll cry myself to sleep.

Sunday 8 September

Michael gave me a new spoon.

All's forgiven.

If Uri bends this one, I'll bend him!

Friday 13 September

Michael told me he's thinking of sending me to
school in January.

The local kindergarten to be precise! I think it
sounds a bit crackers, but I'll give anything a go. If
nothing else, I might come to understand children
– helpful when you're living with Peter Pan.

Wednesday 18 September

OH MY GOD, Michael is full of surprises.

Me and Muscles had just finished watching *The
Golden Girls*, an amazing new show about four
older ladies, when Michael came in and told us to
follow him.

'If you like TV, you're gonna *love* this,' he giggled
as we walked (and Muscles slid). Suddenly I was in

a room I'd never noticed before, and staring at the biggest screen I've ever seen.

'Welcome to my private cinema,' smiled Michael. 'Reserved for me and my best friends only. And when it comes to best friends, you two are right up there.'

Me and Muscles looked at each other and smiled. What a sweetie my dear pet MJ could be. I looked around. At the back of the room stood a popcorn machine, and a counter stuffed with Gummi Bears, Hershey's, Twizzlers, Lifesavers, Baby Ruths and potato chips.

'Candies!' said Michael before demolishing a Baby Ruth. 'They're delicious. Knock yourselves out.'

I grabbed a chocolate bar. It was my first Baby Ruth (until then I hadn't gone much further than banana splits), and it was divine. Such sweetness I had never experienced, and within ten minutes I'd sampled every delight on offer.

The sugar rush was like nothing on earth – Lord knows how many bananas I would have to eat to get that high. Talk about a short cut to sugar oblivion – candy is something else. Muscles didn't muck around either – he slammed down so many Lifesavers he was twitching all over.

We spent the whole day watching film after film, kicking off with *Healthy, Wealthy and Dumb*, a Three Stooges film. Michael said he's seen all of their films hundreds of times, and I have to say Curly, Larry and Moe had me rolling in the aisles.

Then onto *Singin' In The Rain* – a revelation. MJ's obsessed with Gene Kelly, and I can see why – Michael's raindance the other night wasn't a patch on Mr Kelly's umbrella work.

And then there was Debbie Reynolds – let's just say watching her move set an embarrassing part of me moving too. I think I noticed Muscles tensing up a bit as well.

Thursday 19 September

Yesterday was truly wonderful, but I'm feeling
pretty rough after all that candy.

What goes up has to come down, I suppose, and
man am I *low* on sugar. There's only one thing for
it – more! – but the cinema door is locked and MJ's
out of town for a couple of days. Balls.

I've gone through all my bananas, and those
sugared almonds just ain't hitting the spot no more.
All I can do is sleep it off.

Friday 20 September

Woke up early with nightsweats after delirious
dreams – something about Liz Taylor, Diana Ross
and lots of melted chocolate.

I don't remember many clothes being involved.

What I wouldn't do for some more candy – and
more dreams.

Saturday 21 September

I thought I *was* dreaming when Michael came home today.

Me and Muscles were waiting to greet him. I was wearing a delightful Versace dressing gown (Muscles remained as nature intended), but when Michael came through the door I gasped and nearly fell over with shock (Muscles nearly rolled): dear little Mikey's delicate nose was *covered* with bandages; his chin too.

He looked like he'd been to hell and back, but said hello casually enough.

'*Never mind "hello"*,' I screamed. '*What on earth happened, Michael?*'

'Someone must have beaten him up,' hissed Muscles, curling up with fury. 'If I ever get my body on them I'll squeeze them to death.'

Tears flooded my eyes and I jumped up to hold my beloved pet. Michael looked like an Egyptian Mummy after a very long night out. It was

108

---

heartbreaking to think what had happened to MJ in my absence.

'*I should never have let you go alone,*' I wailed. '*This will never happen again, mark my words.*'

Michael must have sensed my upset. 'I guess you're wondering about my face,' he said, sitting me down on nearest chaise longue. 'It's not what it looks like, so don't worry. I've had a little work done, that's all.'

He didn't explain any further, but it meant the world to know Michael was OK. We spent the rest of the day cuddled up in the cinema watching Disney films (and loading up on candy again – those Twizzlers are right on the money). Was transfixed by *Mary Poppins* (that Dick Van Dyke has a funny way of talking, though) and *Pinnochio* was amazing – loved the way the little guy's nose got bigger when he lied, and smaller when he told the truth.

Hope Michael was telling the truth about his face. Whatever does he mean by 'work'?

Sunday 22 September

Another day, another candy comedown.

I really overdid it on the Reese's Cups yesterday – by the time Mary Poppins began singing 'A Spoonful of Sugar' I was already on cloud nine. Paying the price for it now.

Muscles could tell I was down, and tried to cheer me up with a joke: What did Tarzan say when he saw 500 elephants coming over the hill? 'Look, 500 elephants are coming over the hill'.

Didn't get it.

Muscles is quite dry sometimes, and I'm too embarrassed to ask him to explain.

Elephants and hills aside, I know what I'd do if Tarzan came on TV: turn it off. I've got no time for the fella, nor that Cheeta. So what if the ape can stand in front of the camera and ring a bell? A *monkey* could do that. You want good acting, try Julie Andrews.

110

Tuesday 24 September

I can feel my sugar problem escalating.

Spent another day in the cinema, but this time I was on my own. I'm ashamed to admit I ate so much candy I nearly brought it all up again. Eating so much alone can't be right, but I can't help chasing that buzz.

Watched *Snow White and The Seven Dwarfs*.

Not bad, but I must say the bit where the wicked stepmother asks the mirror, 'Who is the fairest one of all?' made me think of Michael. Not that he's wicked or anything, but he does spend an awful amount of time in front of the mirror – he's even started plucking his eyebrows!

Some might call it vanity, but I see it as insecurity. Bless his white cotton socks. Still, if it makes him happy, that's fine by me.

A good day. Must cut back on the candy though – stocks are running low too.

Sunday 28 September

Met Latoya today, though at first I thought it was Michael with a couple of balloons down his T-shirt.

They look so alike, but their chests certainly differ.

She's got a funny little nose, just like her brother – it's nothing like the old photos in the picture gallery. What a bizarre family. I'd love to know the what's up with those noses. Latoya seems nice enough – she and Michael seem very close.

1986

Wednesday 1 January

My new year's resolution is to cut down on the candy.

Since I last wrote, my little sugar problem has gone from bad to worse. Suffice to say, I have piled on the pounds and the night sweats have become unbearable. For the next month it's bananas and nuts for Bubbles.

I'll reintroduce the candy in moderation after that.

113

Christmas came and went, but we didn't celebrate it – Michael's a Jehovah's Witness and they don't do that sort of thing. Bah, humbug, I say (but only because I sneaked a peek at *A Christmas Carol*).

Thursday 2 January

Michael wasn't kidding when he said I'd be going to kindergarten!

I start next week. Nervous to be honest, and not quite sure why I'm being sent to hang out with a load of kids. You wouldn't pack a little kid off to the jungle, after all. Mind you, I'm a pretty smart chimp.

I'll probably run rings around them.

Monday 6 January

My first day at school.

Had to be up early (I've taken to sleeping in,

these days) to get to kindergarten school for 10 o'clock. Michael helped me dress – blue overalls and a pair of Kickers seemed like a good idea. Understated. School is no place for Versace garb, after all.

Mike and I hopped in the Rolls Royce and set off. Mike must have sensed my nerves, for I was unusually quiet in the car, and had completely lost my appetite.

'You're gonna love it, Bubs. Kids are great,' he reassured me.

How wrong he was.

At first glance, my classmates seemed anything but great. When MJ led me into the classroom, it was sheer pandemonium. I've never seen so many little people running in so many directions at once. Some were laughing, some were crying, others were just making as much noise as humanly possible. I couldn't believe Michael thought this would be my scene.

What a drip.

A teacher came in, and within a few seconds order had been restored. Once everyone had shut up, Mrs P introduced me to the class, who stared at me like I was some kind of freak show. She told them I was here to learn, and that I was a very nice chimp – nice of her to say so, but a little assuming of her considering we'd never met.

I spent the rest of the day fending off the hands of 30 children. It seemed they could think of nothing better to do than 'pat Bubbles', as Mrs P put it. Talk about invasion of personal space – it was horrendous.

Can't a chimp get on with his colouring in without a three-year-old's hand on his head?

By the time I got home I was frazzled, and the only thing I'd learned is that kids are fairly stupid. MJ reckons he missed out on his childhood, huh? Well, if colouring in and making a racket are what childhood's all about, then he didn't miss much. OK, I'm being a little insensitive, but I'm in a bad mood.

I am stressed out.

Forget my diet, I'm off to find some candy.

Tuesday 7 January

School again.

Hanging out with a bunch of kids on a sugar comedown ain't all that. Enjoyed a bit of painting though – drew a picture of Michael dressed up in a spoon outfit and bending Uri Geller's arm. Cheered me up, but Mrs P looked a little worried.

Mrs P went through the fire drill at school. In case of fire we have to line up in single file from the smallest to the tallest. Suits me fine, obviously, but I don't see the logic of it.

Do tall people burn slower?

Wednesday 8 January

This school lark is turning out to be rather a laugh after all.

The lessons are a little dull (Mrs P keeps banging on about the alphabet, but Michael taught me my ABC *ages* ago – it really is as easy as 1-2-3) but I've been injecting a bit of fun into the lessons. During this morning's alphabet, I jumped onto my desk, did a spin and broke into a howling rain dance. The kids loved it, and I think Mrs P was impressed.

She obviously thinks I'm going to be famous – she said if I mess around much more I'm going to be history.

Thursday 9 January

I got in a fight with Timmy, this really annoying kid at school – kept calling me a monkey.

Teacher said it was six of one and half a dozen of the other.

How ridiculous. There were only two of us.

Friday 10 January

It seems school's out for Bubbles.

I'd just put my overalls and Kickers on this morning when Michael told me he'd decided kindergarten might not be quite right for me. He's probably right – I think I was stealing the limelight from Mrs P, and I wasn't learning much.

So it's out with the overalls, and back to Versace. What a chameleon I am.

Saturday 11 January

Had a lie-in, took a long bath, and put on my favourite robe – a divine sequinned Versace number that made me look quite the man about the house.

Came downstairs to find Liz Taylor sitting in the

kitchen with Michael. My heart fluttered with joy. How I'd pined for Liz since our first encounter. There is a God, I thought, as I approached Liz for a kiss. She bent down to embrace me and I got a good look at her magnificent bosoms. I shuddered with delight as she held me.

I could have stayed there for all eternity.

'Bubbles, you look superb,' beamed Liz.

'*You're not wrong there, baby, and it's all for you,*' I said (a little white lie never hurts anyone).

'Morning Bubs,' smiled Mike. He seemed so happy around Liz; nothing but a good thing.

'Michael's been spoiling you, hasn't he Bubbles?' said Liz with a wink. 'Michael, if you loved me you'd buy me a robe just like Bubbles. In fact, I'd say you should buy me a mink.'

Michael giggled. 'No problem, Liz, I'll get you a mink if it means that much to you. But there's one condition. You have to keep its cage clean.'

Liz paused for a second, then burst out laughing.

1986

The joke went right over my head, to be honest.
Still, watching Liz heaving with laughter was a
treat. Those bosoms…

'How's the latest romance, Liz?' asked Michael.

'Oh, you know. Men are like bananas. They
older they get, the less firm they are.'

I got that one, alright.

'I think I need an younger man,' mused Liz.
'After all, a hard man is good to find!'

My ears pricked up at this. Maybe there's a
chance for me. I'm young, and certainly one very
firm banana when Liz is around. Luckily she's
staying for a couple of days.

Sunday 12 January

Michael's face bandages came off today.

It didn't take long for me to figure out what he'd
meant by 'a little work.'

My pet's been butchered!

His nose is even *thinner* than before, and someone's taken a chunk out of his chin. When I first saw him in the hall with Liz I nearly went apeshit, but didn't want to act up in front of the woman I loved. There was one thing I wanted to know.

'Why, *man*, *why?*' I said, pointing and scratching my head.

Michael smiled as if everything was *normal*, and Liz didn't look too put out, either.

'How do you like my new look, Bubs?' said Michael.

I was speechless.

'Come on, Bubs,' said Liz, 'Let's go and help Michael with his makeup.'

Whatever, I thought, taking her hand. Anything to spend time with Miss Taylor. Off we marched to the bathroom, and I spent the next half hour watching Liz go to work on Michael. I have to say she did a better job than he would have. She got his eyes just so, but the whole thing bored the hell out of me. I was about to doze off when Liz turned to me.

'I think Bubbles would look exquisite with a bit of eye shadow, don't you Michael?' she said.

I froze as an awful flashback to my science days hit me. Then I began to tremble. Then I thought she might be joking. She wasn't.

'Come on, Bubs, it's just a bit of fun!' she smiled. 'I won't hurt you, promise – I'll be very careful. All you have to do is look down while I put it on...'

It struck me that if I looked down while Liz was in front of me I'd have a clear view of her joyous breasts for a good few minutes. What the hell? I thought, and I was sold in a second. I raised my eyebrows, shrugged and looked down as Liz came towards me.

Oh boy, did I get a good view of those puppies! They jiggled a bit as Liz went to work on my eyes. She was so tender and delicate that it was actually rather pleasant, as was the sensation between my legs (which I quickly crossed to avoid any awkwardness).

'Done!' said Liz after a few minutes. 'You look wonderful'. Nervously I looked in the mirror. What a disaster – there was so much red around my eyes I looked like Ziggy Stardust. But I took it with good grace and grinned at Liz. I didn't want to offend her, so spent the rest of the day with 'It Ain't Easy' in my head. Looking like David Bowie wasn't easy *at all*. I waited til Liz hit the sack, and washed all the red crap off. Never again. Sometimes it's worth sticking to your guns, however tempting an offer may seem.

Monday 13 January

The house felt empty after Liz left.

Me and Mikey skulked around for a bit until he suggested something cheer us up – shopping!

124

Fantastic, I thought, and prayed that our trip would include stopping at a candy store (I'm running dangerously low).

'Take us to Beverly Hills, James,' said Michael as we jumped in the limo. James nodded and started the engine. As we cruised down the drive, I noticed Louis the llama grazing on the lawn (Michael let him out once in a while to cut the grass). I wound the window down and leaned out.

'Keep up the good work, Louis,' I yelled. 'We're off to LA for the day.'

Louis didn't look up, but I knew I'd got him good and proper.

'You and Louis get on well, don't you, Bubs?' said Michael.

Yeah, right, pal. If only you knew.

Visions of Versace, Armani, and Yves Saint Laurent pieces danced before my eyes as the limo sped towards Beverly Hills. I was ready to shop 'til I dropped, and assumed Michael was feeling the

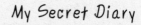

same way. Indeed he was, but only when we pulled up at a massive warehouse did I realise just what he had in mind. We'd stopped outside Toys R Us, of all places. *Toys!* I thought, what the hell…?

'Let's go, Bubbles – this place is heaven!' said Michael as he leaped from the car.

The scene that unfolded beggared belief. A manager escorted Michael around the emporium, and my eyes widened as Michael picked out *thousands* of items. Dolls, cars, games, sports gear – you name it, Michael wanted it. When he ordered 300 Peter Pan figures I began to think he was losing it. I tried to get his attention and put a stop to the madness, but MJ appeared transfixed by his surroundings, lost in a world meant for kids.

Head in hands, I looked on while Michael spent, spent, spent. A couple of hundred Care Bears later, we finally arrived at the checkout.

'That'll be fifty-eight thousand dollars, Mr Jackson. Thank you so much for visiting us again.'

'*Again?*' I yelled. '*How often does this insanity happen?*' (Needless to say, I was ignored.)

'No, thank *you*,' said Michael breezily, and handed over his card. 'I'll see you again in a month.'

So there was my answer. I started to go weak at the knees. Such extravagance I'd never seen. I wondered where on earth Michael was planning to put all this crap. There was no way it would fit in the limo, that was for certain.

Back in the car park, I could only fold my arms and stare at my crazed pet in disbelief.

'What's up, Bubs?' said Michael. 'Was there a toy you wanted, or something?'

Was there *hell*. In no way did I approve of any of this. I pointed at the shop, stomped my feet and wagged my finger at him. Michael put his hand out (we *always* hold hands) but I wouldn't take it. Suddenly, he looked all hurt.

'So, you're angry with me,' he said. 'You think

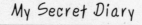
I'm stupid for buying all those toys, right?'

I nodded.

'You think all those toys are for me, do you?'

Another nod from me and Michael began to laugh. 'Shamone, Bubbles, let me explain.'

Whatever Michael had to say, I didn't want to hear it. I stuck my fingers in my ears all the way home, and sulked in the cinema for the rest of the day. I was in no mood for kids' stuff, so watched Clint in *Escape From Alcatraz*. The film made me think about the past, but it also made me consider my current predicament. Michael's nice and all, but Michael's topsy-turvy world is starting to feel like a crazy sort of prison.

What a day.

All those toys, all that expense. I'll go to Toys R Us again over my dead body. And what's the backwards 'R' all about anyway?

What a mad world.

Tuesday 14 January

How dumb I feel.

When I told Muscles all about yesterday, he explained that Michael had bought the toys for poor children. He sends them as gifts all over the world. Muscles had seen it all before – apparently the budget's around $1 million a year.

I felt terrible.

I'd been awfully mean to MJ yesterday, and needed to make it up to him ASAP. I soon came up with a plan. I went to the bedroom, dug out the pirate costume he'd tried to put me in months back, and put it on. If Michael wanted to play Peter Pan, I'd let him.

Michael was over the moon. 'Oh my God, it's Captain Hook,' he exclaimed when he saw me. 'I guess you've figured out the toy thing, then.'

We spent the afternoon engaged in battle – and Captain Hook let Peter win of course. It was the least I could do for dear Mikey.

At bedtime, I discovered my crib had been filled with regurgitated grass. It took me a second to figure out who was responsible – that bloody lawnmowing llama!

What goes around comes around, I guess.

Monday 5 May

Been a boring few months.

I can't stop yawning, and have taken to sleeping during the day.

Tuesday 3 June

Something to do at last.

Michael's about to start working on a new album and he wants me to go to the studio with him. Just as well, because there's no way I'd let him go anywhere without me these days.

Look what happened to him the last time I left

him to his own devices – he let someone cut his nose up and stick a dent in his chin.

Wednesday 4 June

Went to the studio with Michael and met Quincy Jones.

Quincy's gonna be the producer on the album. A seriously cool dude; I can't imagine he's into Peter Pan stuff. Me and Quincy hit it off right away, and Michael seemed very at home in a recording environment – for once he acted like a grown up.

Tuesday 1 July

So much for acting like a grown up.

Me and Michael went to a charity bash today, and he wore a surgical mask, a scarf around his neck and a pulled-down fedora hat. What in God's name is he playing at?

So much for all the 'work' he's had done on his face – what's the point if he's not going to let anyone see it?

Wednesday 2 July

Michael's taken to wearing his surgeon's mask around the house.

Does he think he's a doctor or something? If anyone needs an operation, it's him – I'd prescribe some serious surgery on the part of his brain labelled 'common sense'.

Still, I just can't stop loving him.

Thursday 3 July

Michael acting very weird.

It's good to know everything's OK.

1986

Friday 4 July

Watched *The Elephant Man* with Michael.

Very sad film. Put me right off my popcorn.

Michael told me he identifies with the main character. I don't quite see why – The Elephant Man can't help the way he looks.

Michael *can*.

Wednesday 30 July

Haven't seen Diana Ross for a while.

I miss her lovely legs. I was listening to 'Ain't No Mountain High Enough' for old time's sake, when Michael told me he'd had a bit of a tiff with Diana earlier on in the year. MJ had been due to dine with Diana at some posh place in Beverly Hills, but had ended up inviting Diana to join him and Liz Taylor somewhere else instead. I don't understand. When I sit down to eat, I couldn't give two hoots who gets there first.

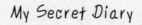

Maybe Michael's been acting weirder than normal because of the Diana thing, or maybe he's just stressing about the new album.

Who knows?

Friday 15 August

Had an interesting-looking delivery today.

A huge piece of gear, I can only describe it as a massive tube made out of metal and glass. Whatever it is, it's a terrifying contraption.

Looks like a torture chamber, and it's sitting right next to the bedroom!

Saturday 16 August

Was woken around 6am by a whirring noise.

Michael was nowhere to be seen. I panicked a little, and ran into the hall to find Michael fast asleep in the tube thing. I rapped hard on the glass.

1986

'*What the hell are you doing in there, you goon?*'
I yelled.

Michael lifted up the glass door and grinned. 'I'm sleeping in a hyperbaric chamber, Bubs!'

'*Speak English, cowboy,*' I said, blinking in the early morning light.

'It's an oxygen tank, Bubs! Perfectly safe – jump in! The oxygen will help you live forever.'

I didn't believe him of course, but jumped in anyway. What a lovely feeling it was breathing all that pure oxygen. I felt pretty good as I drifted off to sleep, and even better when I woke up a few hours later. I don't think I've ever had so much energy. This was better than any sugar rush – I was positively euphoric. I wanted to jump for joy, and before I knew was doing backflips all around the house.

Michael was even more hyper than me – he'd had a good few hours longer in the magic chamber. He sprang out of it, and began dancing like a

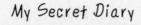

maniac (and there wasn't even any music playing!).
I've never seen anybody dance so fast, or so long
– one spin went on so long the clock struck
twice, and so many 'OWs' were coming out of his
mouth that my dear pet sounded like a friggin'
machine gun.

It was totally awesome.

We danced so hard it was dark before we
stopped. When we eventually looked at the clock,
we realised it was 10pm. Damn, I thought, we
haven't even had *breakfast* yet. Suddenly I was
very tired, and very hungry. I checked the mirror
– I looked like crap. Michael didn't look too good,
either. So much for a machine that makes you
live forever!

If we keep this oxygen lark up, we'll be goners
sooner rather than later.

The machine would have to go.

I took Michael by the hand, led him back to
the chamber, and switched it off. He got the

message – we'd had a good time but I didn't want it to end in tears.

We ate 'breakfast' at midnight, and went back to the bedroom, exhausted.

Too much fun is a dangerous thing.

Tuesday 2 September

Janet came around today.

I've met Michael's sis a few times (gorgeous she is, too) but she's never said that much to me. Michael was busy gelling his hair when Janet showed up, so I thought I'd make her welcome. I held up coffee pot, and raised my eyebrows.

'*Fancy a cuppa Joe, Jan?*' I smiled.

Before she had the chance to reply, Janet's right breast popped out of her bra, and I was faced with a full-on view of a gorgeous ripe nipple. Janet shrieked and ran from the room.

She needn't have been so embarrassed. At least

it happened in the privacy of our own home.

It wasn't like the whole world could see.

Wednesday 3 September

Spent the day with Muscles watching *Lassie* –
what a show. That dog is one cheeky hussy. Little
do the humans know, but she's always ad-libbing
in the rudest possible way, especially when she's
talking to Timmy's dad, Paul. On last week's
episode, she tacked on, '*Boy I could do with some
male company,*' after barking to Paul that Timmy
was caught in a fire. This week, it was even better.
'*Quick, Paul, Timmy's down the well!*' woofed the
old girl. '*But that's not all – I think I might be
pregnant.*'

Lassie obviously got her stud, then. And I
thought *Cheers* was comedy gold.

Lassie is pure genius!

1986

Thursday 4 September

Janet's still here.

She was having a swim this morning and I went out to say 'Hi'. She saw me approaching, smiled and climbed out of the pool.

'Hi Bubbles,' she said, all nice and friendly, but as I opened my mouth to screech her nipple popped out *again*. I could hardly believe it. Unlike the other day, Janet appeared not to notice. Not until she realised how transfixed I was did she cover herself up and sit down.

'Sorry, Bubbles,' she laughed. 'I don't know how that happened again.'

It *was* rather a coincidence. Part of me wonders if Janet's doing it on purpose.

Friday 5 September

She is! No doubt.

This afternoon, Janet walked through the lounge

139

while I was watching *Lassie*, and her nipple had already popped out. She said hello as if nothing was amiss, and left the room. Janet *must* fancy me, surely. I have to admit, I've got some pretty strong feelings for her, but there's no way I could act on them. Getting jiggy with MJ's sis would be wrong in so many ways. Lovely girl, but maybe in the next life. She's leaving tomorrow, so that's OK.

Saturday 6 September

Janet Jackson has left the building.

Phew! Had some very racy dreams last night – all that titillation has really got to me.

Time for a cold bath and a bracing walk.

Wednesday 8 October

Michael is really cracking on with the tracks for the new album. We've been in the studio for weeks.

1986

The days are long and gruelling, but Michael seems to thrive on it. Obviously I'm a huge support. I'm there for him 24/7, always waiting in the wings with a glass of water when the 'hee-hees' start to get a bit too croaky.

Thursday 9 October

Made a bit of a boo-boo at the studio today.

I got so excited watching Michael sing the chorus to *Dirty Diana* that I jumped onto the mixing desk. Mikey was mid lyric when he saw what was happening and shouted 'no' after every 'Dirty Diana'. When the song was finished, we listened back to it and Quincy loved it. The 'no' is staying in! What a team!

Friday 10 October

Still glowing from my contribution to Michael's

songwriting. 'Dirty Diana' is one rockin' song.
Michael won't say who it's about, but I've got a
sneaky feeling Mikey had Miss Ross in mind when
he penned the piece. Man, those lyrics turn me on
(not to mention the thoughts of Miss Ross they
conjure up).

1987

Monday 5 January

The songs are written, and now it's time to start recording.

Christmas was quiet again – Michael very nervous about beating sales on *Thriller* with this album. I must say I'm worried too – after all, *Thriller* broke every record on the planet, so it's a bit of a tall order. Michael is one talented fella, so fingers crossed his latest effort will fly off the shelves.

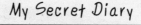

Tuesday 6 January

I don't believe it.

I seriously don't believe it.

After banging on to me about 'potential sales'
of the new album, Michael has gone and totally
shot himself in the foot. I was having a coffee
(my latest buzz – that stuff is *rocket fuel*, man)
with MJ and Quincy Jones in between takes of
'Man In The Mirror' (a more apt song for
Michael I cannot imagine – he spends half his
life gazing at himself, and I wouldn't be surprised
if he makes a change to his nose again at some
point).

The scene unfolded thus:

Quincy: So, Michael, how do you feel
          the album's shaping up?

MJ: It's good Quincy, real good. I'm
          loving it.

Quincy: It's better than good, Michael,

144

	it's great. So what you gonna call it?
MJ:	Well, I've been thinking about this, Quincy, and I like the idea of calling it *Bad*.

(At this point I nearly spat my coffee out)

Quincy: I like it, Michael, I like it very much indeed, my friend.

(At this point I spat my coffee out)

Bad! After mountains of work, vast tracts of time and effort, Michael Jackson, King of Pop, has decided to call his new album *Bad*. Why would he do this to himself? Why would Quincy agree to it? There is only one answer: both of them are one hundred percent certified, bona fide, original brand *loonies*. Excuse my French, but what the friggin'

hell are they thinking? My dear pet's new *tour de force* isn't *bad*, it's good. Very good. Lord give me strength.

I need some candy.

Wednesday 7 January

I'm depressed.

Decided not to go to the studio today. This 'bad' business is doing my head in. If there's some rhyme to their reason, I can't see it. But what do I know – I'm just a chimp. On this occasion, I'm going to bow out and let the 'professionals' do their thing.

Spent the day in the cinema, but didn't watch any films. I just needed to be alone in the darkness with my sweet treats. Michael's had a load of foreign goodies imported – amaretti and almond *biscotti* from Italy are going down a treat, as are stuffed prunes from France. But when it comes to snacking my current *piece de resistance* hails from England: Brandy Snaps. I simply can't get enough of them.

Today I filled 16 snaps with squirty cream from the fridge and lost myself in a brandy-fuelled extravaganza.

Thursday 8 January

Feel much better now.

Michael can do what he wants with the album – I'll stand by him come rain or shine.

Friday 20 March

Martin Scorsese is going to be directing the 'Bad' video – hooray!

I've seen *Taxi Driver* and *Mean Streets*, and they were right up my alley. Marty is one tough mother, and I'm glad he'll be there to knock

Michael into shape. The whole thing was Quincy's idea.

Way to go, Mr Quince.

Saturday 21 March

Bonus – I've been invited along to the set for the filming.

This is great news, as it means I don't have to waste time devising a way to invite myself. Shooting starts Monday.

Can't wait.

Sunday 22 March

It seems someone somewhere thinks I'm not toilet-trained.

Apparently I have no choice but to wear a *nappy* if I want to go on set tomorrow. What do they think I'm gonna do, crap on the cameraman? How

insulting. Michael knows full well I can use a toilet as well as any man. Oh, well, I suppose I can put up and shut up for a few days if it's a choice between working with Marty or watching *Lassie* home alone.

Monday 23 March

Where do I start? Today was awesome.

Met Martin Scorsese, for one, and spent the day being pampered by a huge film crew. I wowed them with a string of virtuoso backflips (step aside, Cheeta – daddy's home now), clapping and somersaults, not forgetting to throw in a few well-executed moonwalks. I think Michael was a little put out to be honest. I think he realised I was the star of the show today.

Tuesday 24 March

Back on set.

The cast showed up today – what a bunch of bad boys. Mean looking fellas from the 'hood, the lot of them. I think I'm starting to understand why Michael's chosen _Bad_ for an album name.

I was a little bit intimidated to be honest, and glad of my nappy…

Wednesday 25 March

This nappy is starting to give me gyp.

It's a little uncomfortable, and rather large. I have to keep adjusting it on set, and I think some of the guys think I'm playing with myself. Marty certainly gave me a funny look, but I just fixed him with my best De Niro glare, and he averted his eyes.

Who's the tough guy now, Marty?

1987

Thursday 26 March

Michael noticed me fiddling with my crotch, and
started impersonating me, which made us both
laugh.

Then, to my complete amazement, he
incorporated it into his dance moves during
filming. I've never seen him grab himself so much.
He must think I look pretty cool.

Either that, or he's wearing a nappy too.

Friday 27 March

This 'Bad' video is hot.

Michael plays a hard man sorting out a gang war,
although he doesn't look as mean as the rest of the
cast. Bless him, he's such a gentle soul.

He wouldn't say boo to a goose – but he'd
probably say hi and offer it a place to live.

Friday 29 May

OK, we're back in weirdsville again.

This time Michael's really on the edge – he's only gone and offered $1 million to the London Hospital Medical College for a load of *bones*. Apparently the hospital own the skeleton of John Merrick, the guy from *The Elephant Man*, and for some reason MJ wants them in his living room. Frankly, I don't see how a bag of bones would make much of a centre-piece. In an effort to distract him, I showed MJ a lovely looking floral vase in the Macy's catalogue (limited run, and very tasteful too), but he wasn't having any of it. Mikey wants dem bones, and that's that.

Personally, I reckon anyone who's prepared to spend a million big ones on vertebrae is a bonehead.

Saturday 30 May

The papers are going nuts over this bone story, and
Michael's loving every minute of it.

They've given him a new nickname: Wacko
Jacko (Wacko for short). Suits him perfectly.
Flicking through the cuttings, I noticed a line
about Michael supposedly having asked Lizzy
Taylor to marry him. Hilarious – and a load of tosh.
Honestly, journalists these days are so slack with
their research. It wasn't Wacko who proposed to
Liz, *it was me!* I'd had a few too many Brandy
Snaps a few weeks back, and got down on one knee
with a gold ring I'd fashioned from a chocolate
coin wrapper. Needless to say Liz declined my offer.
I'm glad, actually, as she seems to go through
husbands faster than I go through Twinkies.

Once Michael asked Liz to tell me how many
men she'd tied the knot with.

'What is this?' replied Liz. 'A memory test?'

153

Monday 27 July

'I Just Can't Stop Loving You' (a song about me, of course) has finally been released, and boy, sales are going crazy.

It's the first single from *Bad* and it's going to be number one *everywhere*. Michael's obviously delighted – we're having a huge party to celebrate the launch. I've already chosen my outfit – a very flattering trousers-braces combo. Versace, of course.

Can't wait.

P.S. Michael didn't get the Elephant Man's bones. Phew.

Tuesday 28 July

Party time.

Tonight's party was awesome. Anybody who's anybody turned up. What a blur of famous faces. Steven Spielberg and Whoopi Goldberg showed up (both of them shining representatives of the

Berg family). Lionel Ritchie came along (and, thankfully, made no attempt to dance on the ceiling), and I'm sure I saw Dan Aykroyd and Paula Abdul dancing together. Liz and Diana Ross were out in force (I noticed Liz hovering around the buffet for an awfully long time) but the star of the show was definitely *moi*.

Baby, did I work that room.

I've never had so much attention from the ladies (partly down to my exposed hairy chest, I'm sure – those trouser suspenders didn't leave much to the imagination) – and I had to keep making pit stops to wipe the lipstick marks from my face. Everyone stopped and stared when I danced, and I noticed John Travolta taking out a notepad when I came out of a triple spin with a flying kick.

You're never too old to learn, John.

Wednesday 12 August

Something very funny happened today: I received myself in the post.

Muscles received himself too.

Someone's had the bright idea to create stuffed toys of Michael's animals and call them 'Michael's Pets'. Whatever will they think of next. I've a problem with this on two levels. First, I'm *not* Michael's pet; I'm his best friend and second, the stuffed Bubbles looks like a demented freak – I look half-human, half-chimp, and there's this bizarre smile on my pursed lips that makes me look like I'm chewing a wasp and trying to look happy about it. How ridiculous. Muscles looks more like an overgrown worm than a formidable snake.

If anyone's a pet, it's Michael – he's the one who needs looking after.

I bet those cynical toy makers wouldn't go in for a 'Bubbles' Pet' doll though.

Friday 14 August

I'm very worried about Michael.

He's about to go on a world tour and I'm not going with him. How on earth will he cope without me? He knows as well as I that he needs me by his side during pressured times.

I'll miss him, too.

Saturday 15 August

Michael's nervous about leaving for Japan tomorrow.

I tried to take his mind off things with a game of Peter Pan (Muscles even offered to be Tinkerbell), but he wasn't interested. Poor MJ – he said he'd love me to come but he's been advised to go it alone.

Let's just say Muscles and I would love to know who his advisors are.

Sunday 16 August

Saw MJ off at the airport.

I don't do long goodbyes, so we parted quickly. When I got home the house seemed so empty. Sometimes you don't know what you've got 'til it's gone, and I miss him already. I walked around the house looking at all the mad ornaments and gazed longingly at his collection of sequinned gloves. I even tried his Peter Pan outfit on (not quite sure why though; it felt a bit odd). Anyway, I realised none of this crap means anything without Michael. He's the most eccentric, difficult, unfathomable and downright lovely pet in the world and I'm proud to say I love little MJ to bits.

Still, absence makes the heart grow fonder.

Monday 17 August

I miss MJ so bad.

As manly a chimp as I am, I must admit that I

1987

cried myself to sleep last night. What would Clint Eastwood say if he knew? Nothing, I'd guess. He'd probably gaze at the horizon with narrowed eyes and move on.

I wish Michael would call. I stared at the phone for hours today. Nothing.

Come on, Bubbles, stay strong.

Tuesday 18 August

Michael called! And he had fantastic news. Not only does he miss me, he's flying me over to Japan first class. I'd better pack some nappies.

I wonder if they'll let me take Brandy Snaps on the flight?

Wednesday 19 August

In transit – watch out people of Japan, Bubbles is coming to getcha!

This plane is *swanky*. Food's a bit weird though – they keep bringing out all this raw fish. What is it, the chef's day off or something? They call it 'sushi'. Sitting next to some fat bozo from Florida. He's been laying into the Manhattans since we took off. He's just leant over and told me you can tell if you're on a French plane by the hair under the wings.

No idea what he on about.

Thursday 20 August

Touched down in Tokyo this afternoon.

Was a bit of a bumpy landing, mind you – by the time the goddamn plane had stopped, I wasn't sure if we'd landed or been shot down. I emerged from the plane to find 300 journalists and fans waiting for me – 300! What a reception. Turns out Mrs P at kindergarten was right – I am destined for fame. My escorts weaved me silently out of the throng (I've always wanted to do that 'no comment' thing) and into a limo.

Destination: MJ.

Michael ran into my arms when I got to his hotel suite. 'Oh Bubs,' he blubbed, 'I'm so glad you're here. I couldn't do this without you.'

'*No sweat, pal,*' I said, stroking his head. '*I wouldn't have missed it for the world.*'

'It means so much for me to be with the one chimp I know I can trust. Sometimes I think everyone else around me just wants me for my money. You don't love me just because of the fortune I've made performing, do you?'

'*Don't be dumb, Mickey, I'd love ya no matter how you made your money,*' I joked. (Sometimes I'm glad he can't understand me, as he's pretty sensitive. Still, a dumb question deserves a cheeky answer.)

Anyway, I'm back at MJ's side where I belong, and nothing else matters.

I'm knackered from the flight, and need some rest. Big day tomorrow – some press conference with the Mayor of Osaka.

Friday 21 August

Met Mayor Yasushi Oshima for tea. (I was the first animal ever allowed inside the Osaka Town Hall. How important am I!)

Since it was a formal occasion, I wanted to put on the glitz a bit, but MJ was determined we dressed casually. He sported a red shirt and wanted me to match him with some red dungarees and a cream sweater. I wasn't keen when he held up the garb. Michael looked a little crestfallen when I folded my arms.

'It'll look much better on,' he said.

'*Yeah*,' I said. '*On fire. Count me out on this one, buddy.*'

A row ensued, and I ended up conceding. Today

was about Michael after all. Turned out to be a fuss over nothing – they gave us kimonos to put on when we got there. Man, I was loving all that silk. Versace, you are *out*, my friend.

Mayor Oshi was a dude. Nice and short, for a start, so I didn't have to strain my neck too much to look at him, and a really genuine smile. He presented MJ with a 'Key to the City', whatever that is. It looks pretty neat, but I can't see my man Mickey having much use for it – I've never seen him open a door in his life. There's always someone there holding it open for him.

Had a cup of green tea with the Mayor. It's OK, but less of a kick than espresso.

I do miss my cups of Joe.

Saturday 22 August

So much for the city key thing – we didn't even leave the hotel room!

Outside there are hordes of screaming girls desperate to throw themselves all over Mike and me, and what do we do? Nothing, that's what! I swear to God, Michael spent the day putting batteries in toys he'd bought for kids while I waved to all the honeys in the street below. I can't believe Michael spends half his life hanging out with good-looking grannies (no offence to Diana and Liz – I'd kill for a night with either of them) and then ignores *thousands* of babes who'd do *anything* to please him. I bet I could be getting some major action too.

This *sucks*.

Sunday 23 August

Michael's got it into his head that I don't like the smell of cigarette smoke on the walls of our room. He's having them re-papered.

How embarrassing – makes me look like a right

164

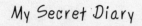

prima donna. The only thing wrong with these walls is that I'm bloody climbing them. I've got cabin fever, and the babes outside just keep on screaming.

Monday 24 August

Got out of the room!

Went to a press conference and did a moonwalk. Golly, I am one famous chimp – saw myself on the TV back in the hotel room.

Eat your amateur little heart out, Cheeta!

Tuesday 25 August

Another press conference.

I'm not sure how much I like this fame game. It's nice being here with MJ and all (I must keep in mind how lonely I was at home without him) but the publicity trail is starting to grate my nerves a little. What I wouldn't give for an afternoon maxing out with Muscles back on the sofa.

Goodness knows what's happening on *Cheers*, and I'm running out of Brandy Snaps.

Friday 26 August

Press conference.

Yawn.

Saturday 27 August

Mikey and I went to Korakuen Stadium for a rehearsal.

I've never seen a bigger building in my life. Apparently 50,000 people are gonna be watching MJ strut his stuff.

Gulp.

1987

Monday 28 August

Jeez, they've really got Michael working day and night.

I had to bow out of the action today. Finished my final Brandy Snap mid-afternoon, and dozed 'til dinner.

Michael and I ate downstairs, for once. Restaurant looked nice, but all they had was sushi (again). Ever heard of a flame grill, guys?

The waiter came over for our order.

'Why don't you have what I choose?' said Michael. I thought that would be unfair. There was no way I was going to leave him hungry. I looked at the menu and pointed to the mackerel.

What a mistake.

I'm in bed as I write, and starving.

Tuesday 29 August

Woke up so hungry I was tempted to eat my kimono.

Instead, I sneaked out of the room, broke into the kitchen and located the fruit. Ten minutes later I'd dispensed with 18 bananas. It was a struggle getting back up the stairs after that lot, but I made it before Michael woke up.

Saturday 12 September

Just back from the most awesome concert ever.

Michael was brilliant, is all I can say. He started with 'You Wanna be Startin' Something', and tore through 18 hits, finishing up with 'Bad'. Michael's crotch got a lot of attention from his hands – the crowd went loopy every time he grabbed himself. I was so proud he'd copied his most successful move from me.

That's my boy, I thought, as I sat there and fiddled with my nappy.

Monday 14 September

Watched the gig again.

Enjoyed it, sure, but not quite as exciting as last night.

Tuesday 15 September

Another day, another concert.

Here's the routine. Mikey takes the stage, people scream for two hours while he sings, and then we got home. Very nice. There's only so much entertainment a chimp can take, and to be honest I'm getting a little bored of the same old, same old.

Friday 18 September

Don't know how Michael does it.

The energy of the man. If I had to do the same act night after night, I'd go mad. Maybe that's why

he *is* mad. Whatever the case, I've had enough of touring already.

Bugger this for a laugh.

Monday 12 October

Man, I am deranged with tiredness and boredom.

Michael's been performing non-stop and coming back exhausted. I'm always there for him, of course, but I've been craving a bit of me time. I've been stuck in this goddamn hotel room for too long. The TV's crap (nothing but a load of Japanese gobbledygook) the food's crap (if I see another raw fish, I'm gonna punch someone) and I've nobody to talk to.

I've really got the blues.

Tuesday 13 October

Hallelujah – I just discovered that the Japan tour is over.

1987

Michael's final show was last night, and now he's off to Australia. The good news is I won't be with him – I'm going back to the US of A. Home sweet friggin' home. When Michael told me I was so excited I exploded into my nappy. Within 24 hours I will be on the sofa next to Muscles.

Michael is so kind – he's obviously picked up on the fact that touring ain't my bag, and doesn't have the heart to drag me around any more. I admire his stamina, I really do, and I'll miss him.

But I won't miss being on the road.

Wednesday 14 October

So long Japan.

See you in the next life (hopefully you'll have discovered flame grilling by then).

171

My Secret Diary

Thursday 15 October

It's oh-so-nice to go travelling, but it's so much nicer to come home. Never a truer word spoken. Arrived back to a fully stocked candy bar and a big squeeze from Muscles.

Famous though I am, my needs are few.

I'm happy.

1988

Saturday 7 May

Michael's been touring for months, and now he's halfway around America.

There must be some serious cash rolling in, because he's treated himself to a new house. A $17 million ranch, to be precise. I think he made the decision partly because he wants a bit more space (2,400 acres should do the trick) and partly because he's off his rocker.

173

I mean, sev-en-teen *million*.

I dread to think how many Brandy Snaps I could buy with that. I could probably snap up the entire factory. Michael seems very happy though, so that's the main thing. He's been getting everything ready for a while, and we're moving in a couple of days! Must make sure he packs the popcorn machine.

Thinking about it, I hope to God there's a cinema.

Sunday 8 May

Michael's just finished the American leg of the tour – he's been *everywhere* and I haven't seen much of him.

I assumed he'd be pleased to be home, and was looking forward to watching a bit of Julie Andrews with him. That turned out to be wishful thinking – he got back today in a foul mood (rare for him). Didn't take long to get to the root of the problem – he's livid that Madonna has won some Artist of the

Decade award. I've never seen him so sulky. OK, Michael's got more talent on the tip of his ruined nose than Madonna's got in her entire body (that's my opinion, anyway), but I don't sit about whinging about Cheeta's underserved fame, do I?

Well, not much.

Madonna Schmadonna. I wish Michael would move on. Perhaps it would be good if we took a holiday...

Monday 9 May

Moving day.

Michael, me and Muscles took a helicopter to Santa Barbara County, and my eyes nearly popped out when I saw Michael's new pad – I've never seen a bigger house.

'Welcome to Neverland,' beamed MJ as we stepped down from the 'copter into a field. We were some distance from the house.

175

'*Oh quit the Peter Pan crap, Michael,*' I said.
'*You're a big boy now – this is a ranch fit for a man.
Why don't we leave all the fairy nonsense in the past,
where it belongs, huh?*'

'Finally, we are in a place where we can be
children forever,' continued Michael, starry eyed
and oblivious.

'*Whatever you say, Buster,*' I shrugged. I glanced
at Muscles and we giggled.

'You gotta love the guy,' said Muscles. 'He may
be one sandwich short of a picnic, but he means
well.'

It was a good point. I gazed at Michael, who
seemed lost in dreamy happiness. I hadn't seen him
look so relaxed in years – his hand was gloveless,
and he wore a simple white T-shirt with black
trousers. Suddenly, it hit me: finally MJ felt at
home. He had a place to call his own. If naming
his ranch after some fairy tale was his idea of
sensible, who was I to get in his way? Overcome

176

with emotion, I jumped up and held my one and only pet MJ.

'*I love you, dude*,' I gushed. '*And I'll be your Captain Hook forever. And Muscles will be your Tinkerbell, won't you, Musky?*'

Muscles nodded and wrapped himself around Michael's legs.

'Come on guys, let's go,' shouted Michael. 'Neverland, ho!'

Joyfully, we bounded across the field. There were trees as far as the eye could see, a beautiful lake and a waterfall, and lush grass everywhere. Paradise. We emerged from a thicket of trees and, suddenly, I understood why Michael was so excited.

Neverland is a dream come true (for Michael, at least, but I admit I love it too). Talk about having Disneyland in your back yard – this place is off the hook. There's a Ferris wheel, a carousel, a zipper, an octopus ride, a rollercoaster, bumper cars and even a swinging pirate ship. But best of all there's *the*

biggest rope swing I've ever seen. My jaw hit the floor when I spotted in hanging from a majestic oak tree. It must be about 30 feet long, and the seat is made of gold – *gold*! I was truly stunned.

'All for you,' winked Mikey. It was easily the best present I've ever had. I snapped out of my trance and jumped on. Muscles wound himself around the rope and MJ gave us an almighty push (he's pretty tough for a little fella).

I've never swung so well – I'm talking *major* air, here. Higher and higher we flew, my eyes filling with water as we whipped through the air. I could tell my centre parting was all over the place, but I didn't give a damn. I screeched with joy.

What a life, I thought.

What. A. Life.

Tuesday 10 May

Slept like a baby last night.

1988

My new crib is twice as big as the last one, and
sits in the corner of Michael's *enormous* bedroom.
Needless to say, Michael was already decked out in
a brand new Peter Pan outfit, and ready for our first
full day of make-believe.

Frankly, I felt the same way.

I quickly transformed myself into Captain Hook
and woke up Muscles. I had a surprise for him – a
glittering pink garter and a wand. (Michael gave
them to me because he thought I'd have a better
chance of persuading a boa constrictor into
costume. Muscles had always gone along with the
Tinkerbell act, but never really got into character.
This was his opportunity to do so with style.)

I won my favourite snake over easily enough (I
promised we would watch *Tarzan* for the next
month, even when *Lassie* was on), and the three of
us spent the morning darting around the
amusement park. We must have looked pretty
insane, but what did we care – we were in

179

Neverland, and there wasn't a soul for miles around. Being Captain Hook was a lot more fun now that I had my own pirate ship.

Mikey and I had an *awesome* swordfight while the vessel swung to and fro. The only problem was Tinkerbell got seasick. Poor old Muscles, he went pretty green (he also looked rather ridiculous holding the magic wand in his mouth!)

Peter Pan won the day, of course. Triumphant, Michael grinned and hugged us.

'Right,' he said. 'Let's go and say hi to the others.'

The others? I thought, staring at Muscles. What was he on about?

'This way to the zoo,' yelled MJ, already running.

To be honest, when we left Encino I'd completely forgotten about the others. My encounters with Louis the llama had put me off going near the place for a long time. Following Michael, I was a little worried I'd get a frosty reception.

1988

I was wrong.

The new zoo was so much bigger, and when I got there everyone appeared *seriously* chilled out.

I hovered in the background while Michael ran in and gave all the animals a hug. Petunia looked about as happy as a pot-bellied pig can look (they do have unfortunate faces, don't they?), and Linus's wool was resplendent in the sun – she baaed with pleasure as MJ gave her a squeeze. Jabbar the giraffe appeared to be in seventh heaven as he took his pick of leaves from the luscious trees, and Mr Tibbs looked absolutely ram-tastic.

And then there was one – Louis the llama.

To my astonishment, Louis greeted me with a friendly yawn.

'Oh, it's you,' he said. He was a little off-hand, sure, but at least the biting sarcasm was gone. 'Been a while, old boy. What say we let bygones be bygones and try to get along? New leaf and all that. This place is rather lovely, after all. Be a shame to

ruin it with hard feelings, wouldn't it, my dear little monkey?'

'Indeed it would,' I said (I let the monkey thing go. Sometimes you've got to turn things around in your head, and I decided to allow Louis his little joke). 'I'm prepared to wipe the slate clean, Louis. And I think it would make Michael very happy to see us getting along – he's very fond of you, you know.'

It was a deal. For the first time since I'd known him, Louis smiled. I entered the enclosure and greeted everyone. I told them all about my adventures with Mikey over the past few years, and they listened intently.

'Quite the celebrity, aren't we?' said Jabbar, with a wink.

'Well, I suppose so,' I said, hoping I wasn't blowing my own trumpet.

'Can't say I envy you, but well done. Someone needs to look after dear Michael, and you seem to have done a formidable job.'

I blushed a little. I didn't know what to say. 'Well, I…'

'…Yes, good on you, Bubbles', chorused Mr Tibbs. 'He looks very happy to me.'

I blushed some more. '*No*, it's not me, not at all.' I looked at Michael. Indeed he did look happy. Was I really anything to do with that? I wondered. I wasn't sure, just then.

As I write this while Michael snoozes by my side, I think the answer may be 'yes'. Perhaps I have made my pet superstar a little happier than he was before. And he's given a lot to me too. In fact, I don't think I could be any happier.

Wednesday 11 May

Correction: today I am happier.

I'm not just happy, I'm on fire with rapturous joy. I've had the kind of day most chimps only ever dream of. It all began quite unremarkably.

'I've got a surprise for you,' said Michael after breakfast. Now I'm back on bananas trying to lose some weight, and for a second I was concerned he was about to lead me to a new shipment of Brandy Snaps. I couldn't have been more wrong. Michael took my hand and led me through the house to the lounge doors.

'Open them,' said Michael with a grin.

The beautiful scene on the other side of those doors was a sight for very, *very* sore eyes. Standing in a line were five of the cutest, juiciest looking chimpesses I have ever seen – *five* girls, each and every one perfect in her own way, all of them the definition of sex on legs. To top it all off, they were dressed as maids.

Is this for real? I wondered. I stood there gawping and pinched myself. It was real, alright.

'Bubbles, say hello to your new staff,' beamed Michael. 'These fine ladies have come all the way from Britain to live with us. They're going to

help clean the house, and I'd like you to manage the team.'

The girls giggled shyly as I surveyed them. I've died and gone to heaven, I thought, I really have. I was speechless.

'That OK with you, Bubs?' said Mike.

'OK?' I grinned. 'OK? *Michael, my man, are you crazy? This is the opportunity of a lifetime. I am honoured. I'll manage these princesses like nobody's ever managed them before. Trust me, man, I will go well beyond the call of duty for these little honeys.*'

I nodded at Michael. He smiled at me so innocently that I wondered if he had any idea just what he'd done for me. 'OK,' he said. 'Well I've got to go out, so I'll leave you to it. The dusters are in the cupboard, Bubs. Good luck!'

And so it began. Michael left us alone and the girls ran over to me immediately.

'We're so glad to meet you, Bubbles,' said a delicious little minx with a pink bow in her hair.

'We've seen you on the TV so many times, and you're soooo cute! I'm Milly, by the way.'

'A pleasure, Milly,' I smiled, kissing her hand. 'And what names do the rest of you lovely ladies go by?'

'I'm Molly,' said a petite vixen, shyly fluttering her long dark eyelashes. 'And this is Dolly,' said Molly (pointing at Dolly) a drop-dead gorgeous brunette with a saucy glint in her eye and two little pigtails in her hair.

'I'm Polly,' chirped a game-looking angel with a perfect little button nose. 'I don't believe you've met my twin sister, Deirdre.'

Twins, I thought, it doesn't get any better than this. I turned to Deirdre. Sure enough, she was identical to her sister, but there was something about the way she held herself that made her seem to be nothing less than a vision. A tall, simmering hottie with deep brown, sultry eyes, she was so hot, I swear I could hear the ground sizzling beneath her feet. But why *Deirdre*? What about all the illys and ollys?

Deirdre's steamy eyes pierced mine for about a minute before she spoke. 'Hey, big Bubba,' she purred. 'What say we all clean the bedroom first? They can be awfully *dirty* places, can't they?'

A sweat broke in the nape of my neck and I felt myself begin to tremble. My throat went dry. 'Yes,' I stammered, 'I suppose they can. Good idea, Deirdre.'

Her gaze remained fixed on me.

'Right girls,' I said, clearing my throat, 'The dusters are in the cupboard at the end of the hall, and the bedroom's right next door.'

'Right you are, Bubbles,' said Dolly. 'We'll get on with it then. Feel free to come check on us whenever…'

With that they tottered out of the room in single file, their perfect little behinds just visible beneath their uniforms. Deirdre turned at the door. 'Don't be long, Bubbsy,' she said with a wink.

My Secret Diary

I had to take a seat. I had to think everything through. I could hardly believe that Michael had just left me in charge of five drop-dead-gorgeous angels from England, *and now they were waiting for me in his bedroom*. It felt too good to be true, but it *was* true. Was Deirdre really hinting at what I thought she was hinting at? Of course she was. My time has come, I thought, Experience beckons at last.

'Well, what the hell are you waiting for, bozo?' I said out loud. 'Get in there!'

I took a deep breath as I paced down the corridor, threw the door wide open and smiled. 'Boss is here, girls,' I said rakishly. 'How are we doing?'

We were doing just fine. On the floor lay five uniforms, and on the bed lay five very naughty young ladies.

'What do we have we here?' I said, stepping out of my dungarees.

The girls tittered and squealed with delight.

'Dive in, big boy,' beckoned Deirdre.

And that's just what I did. Mamma-bloody-Mia. Those British girls are something else.

Thursday 12 May

Spent the morning thinking about yesterday, and spent the afternoon repeating yesterday.

Boy oh boy oh *boy*.

Friday 13 May

Friday 13th – unlucky for some.

Not for me.

After another fine performance all round, we all got chatting. Turns out the girls used to do tea adverts on British telly. Some company called PG Tips. Don't know what 'PG', means, but there's one thing my ladies don't need: Bedroom Tips.

Hot *damn!*

Saturday 14 May

I am aching in a very *good* way.

What a week.

Sunday 15 May

Didn't see the ladies today, Sunday being a day of rest and all that.

Hung out with MJ instead. He's very happy with the state of the house. ('Those girls really know what they're doing', said MJ as he looked around. I could only agree.) We'd just finished a game of Monopoly (MJ's favourite) when Michael told me he had some bad news.

'I couldn't get you a visa for the UK,' he said, a tear in his eye.

I had no idea what he was on about.

'You won't be able to come to England with me,' he explained. 'I'm so sorry, Bubs.'

I can't say I wasn't relieved. Japan was good life

190

experience, but the idea of touring again just didn't swing my rope. Besides, being in the land of the Brandy Snap could well ruin my banana regime.

'*Don't sweat it, superstar,*' I said, trying not to smile. '*Why would I want to go to Britain when I've got five little pieces of it in my back yard?*'

It was true. Now that I'd found my true calling in life ('managing' chimpesses) the idea of press conferences and hotel rooms had lost its (limited) lustre.

'I'll miss you, Bubs,' said Michael. 'And I'll miss Neverland too.'

'*Well, them's the breaks, MJ,*' I said. '*You'll be back in no time, and Captain Hook will be waiting with open arms.*'

So there it is. Michael's off on tour and I'm not going. Life moves on. Anyway, I can't be there to hold MJ's hand forever.

Maybe the boy will do a bit of growing up if I'm not around.

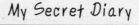

Tuesday 17 May

I bid goodbye to MJ at the gates of Neverland, and scampered up to the zoo to join the ladies.

My harem has their own enclosure, and I'm moving in. That way the house stays clean, leaving more time for rumpy-pumpy. While the pet's away, the owner shall play.

Bring it on, I say.

1989

Friday 27 January

Michael's back.

The *Bad* tour is officially over. After nine months of nonstop loving, I'm pretty shagged out. It's been a wonderful trip on the love train, but my main man is back and I've got to face up to my responsibilities again.

It is great to see Michael again, but his skin causing me concern. He's getting whiter and

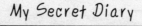

My Secret Diary

whiter, and I just don't get it. Weirder still, he's walking around with a friggin' umbrella *even when it's not raining*. It all started this morning – a perfectly nice sunny day – while we took a walk around the ranch. When I saw the umbrella, I scratched my head and pointed at it quizzically. MJ perceived my confusion and explained he's been diagnosed with lupus and vitiligo. One makes him sensitive to light and the other makes his skin lighter. Hence the whitening and the umbrella.

Mikey had a good time in Britain. Met some dude called Prince Charles and his wife Princess Diana. They were at Wembley Stadium when she told him she loves 'Dirty Diana'. I can quite believe it, too – Michael showed me a photo of her and she does look like a bit of a good-time girl (weirdly, she reminds me of Deirdre). I saw a snap of Charlie, too – now there's one strange-looking mother. His ears are nearly as big as mine!

He's done mighty well to bag Dirty Di, I must say.

194

1989

Sunday 29 January

Came across Michael's tour bag and found tubes
labelled 'Hydroquinone – Skin Whitener'.

Hmmm.

Monday 27 February

Never let it be said that Lizzie Taylor is no oil
painting, because she is.

Literally.

Came downstairs this morning to find Michael
and Liz in the hall admiring a *huge* painting of my
generously-proportioned dream girl. Boy, do those
puppies look big in the painting. Walking past that
every day without getting overexcited is going to
be hard, but hopefully not *too hard.*

It was wonderful to see Liz again. I rushed into
her arms, and forgot all about my five princesses for
a few seconds. I love those girls, but Liz is *all*
woman, and I'm still a sucker for her.

195

Thanks to the girls, I'm getting what I've needed for so long, but there'll always be a place in my heart (and my bed) for Liz.

Tuesday 28 February

I'm tired as hell.

Last night I sneaked out of the bedroom and down to the zoo for an evening of pleasure with Deirdre. She's one steamin' date, but I feel a little guilty. As we made passionate love, I found my mind wandering to wicked thoughts of Liz. I'm sure Deirdre would be heartbroken if she knew.

Liz too, unfortunately.

Wednesday 1 March

Liz's painting is now surrounded by several more paintings and photos.

There's even a rug with the old girl's face on it,

and some film memorabilia. It's a friggin' *shrine*.

Ah, Michael, you're a funny little fruitcake.

Thursday 2 March

Speaking of fruitcakes, Liza Minelli paid a visit today.

I've met Liza before at parties, but never really spent any 'quality' time with her. Boy, is she off the wall – it doesn't matter what you say, she just won't stop smiling.

'Ah Bubbles, schweety, how *are* ya?' beamed Liza when I walked in for breakfast. She grabbed my cheeks and gave them a friendly squeeze.

Frankly, I wasn't in the mood, and managed little more than a shrug in response. (Deirdre accused me of 'being distant' during sex last night, and we had a massive row. She suspects I've been thinking of Liz).

'Ah, shucks, you know you're just sensational, Bubsch, schen-*sshational*!'

197

What the crap is she on about? I thought. I haven't done *anything* yet.

'What say just you and me go have a swell time at some sizzlin' Broadway joint, Bubsch?' she gushed, her red-lipped smile at full stretch, her gleaming set of choppers dazzling my eyes. 'Now whaddya say to that? I'm Judy Garland's daughter, don't you know.'

'*Listen, Lady,*' I said, '*I don't know what you want from me, but it's ten in the morning and I haven't had a coffee yet, so cool it, will ya?*'

Liza took no notice. Suddenly she threw her arms out and her head back. 'Come taste the wine!' she yelled, her smile so wide I thought her face was gonna split.

'*You what?*' I replied, frowning.

'Come blow your horn!' she screamed, eyes sparkling and wild.

'OK, *take it easy, sweetheart.*'

'Life is a cabaret, old Bubbles!'

198

'*Is that so?*' I said over my shoulder as I put the coffee on. '*Are you sure I can't get you a doctor?*'

I looked back at Michael giggling into his umbrella (he's even using one indoors now, God help him). I got the feeling he'd seen all this before. Liza held the outstretched pose for a few seconds and did some weird shake before launching into a full throttle rendition of '*Cabaret*'. I watched her numbly and sipped my coffee. Finishing with a flourish, Liza held her smile – which was starting to freak me out – and gazed at me for what felt like an eternity. I assumed she was waiting for applause, so set my cup down and half-heartedly clapped my hands together a couple of times.

'Did ya like it, Bubsch?' she said, her voice laced with uncertainty. 'Did ya, Mein Herr?'

'*Not at all, sweetheart, not at all,*' I said, and clapped some more. '*In fact, do it again and I'll put a rag in ya mouth, you deranged old hen.*'

'Oh, I knew ya'd like it, Schweety, I could have

told ya ya'd tell me ya like it. Ahh, you're as schwell
as they come, Bubsch, you're the best, Mein Herr.'

I couldn't take any more. I ran and I ran, then I
ran some more. At times even a 2,400 acre ranch
can feel claustrophobic.

Friday 3 March

Michael spent the day sitting in a tree, singing.

He calls it his 'giving' tree, and I know not to
disturb him when he's up there. It's the one place
MJ feels at peace with himself and writes his songs.
He's working on something called 'Black or White'
at the moment – a subject close to his heart. Still,
it's nice to see Michael calm up in those branches.

After all, he's out of his tree most of the time.

Saturday 4 March

The girls gave the house a good going over today,

but Polly got a bit heavy-handed with the duster and smashed one of MJ's favourite vases.

It was a tasteless gold and green thing, but Michael loved it. Polly was distraught, so I decided to take the rap. Once the ladies had closed the janitor cupboard and left, I put on my best sorry face and guided Michael to the scene of the crime. He wasn't happy at all, and told me the vase was irreplaceable.

Thank God, I thought, at least he won't have to worry about buying a new one.

Sunday 5 March

Dear Diary, I am confused.

I keep hearing Prince's voice while I'm 'spending quality time' with the chimpesses. It's been going on for weeks, and I've been praying for an end to it. I'm usually in the middle of a smooch when it happens. All of a sudden, I hear Prince whispering the rudest of suggestions in my ear.

'Touch her here, touch her there,' he'll say, or, 'have you ever tried such and such?'

It's nothing short of terrifying – I'm clearly the only one who hears his sexy instructions, and I am somehow compelled to do exactly what he tells me. Equally frightening is how much the man seems to know about pleasing the ladies – I'm driving them wild at the moment. Prince is one dirty demon. But how the hell has he got into my head? Maybe it's not Prince at all. Maybe I'm losing it.

When will it end?

Monday 6 March

Managing a team of cleaners isn't as easy as it sounds (especially when you're romantically involved with every single one of them and Prince won't stop talking dirty to you).

Deirdre in particular is giving me grief. She knows she's my favourite chimpess, and as a result

has been taking liberties in the workplace. Her timekeeping is atrocious, and this goes down terribly with Milly, Molly, Polly and Dolly. I've been turning a blind eye so far, but today took the biscuit. She was over an hour late. I had to make a stand to avoid mutiny from the others.

'Do you know what time we start work here?' I said when Deirdre strolled in. The room went silent. Dusters poised, the girls stared at Deirdre and waited.

'No,' said Deirdre icily. 'Everyone's already hard at it when I get here.'

Ouch.

I couldn't think of a comeback, so walked off in a huff. Perhaps I should steer clear of Deirdre.

I think she's more of a *femme fatale* than a homemaker.

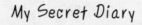

My Secret Diary

Saturday 1 April

'I've got a girlfriend,' said Michael over breakfast.

I spat my banana out and fell off my chair.

'Michael, this is truly amazing news. And who's the lucky lady?'

'Just kidding,' laughed Mike. 'Happy April Fool's day.'

Sunday 2 April

Funny to think I have five girlfriends while Michael has none.

How I wish he'd get one.

I'd love to go on a double date to Disneyland.

Thursday 22 June

I was towelling myself after a thoroughly relaxing mid-afternoon jacuzzi when Michael rushed outside. He was in hysterics, and waving a copy of

1989

The National Enquirer.

'Check this out,' he giggled, and thrust the rag in my hand. Michael hee-heed away like a monkey while I read the headlines: PRINCE USES EXTRASENSORY PERCEPTION TO DRIVE BUBBLES CRAZY.

I was dumbstruck. My towel dropped to the ground as I grabbed the paper with both hands and read the article.

'Of all the crazy shit they've ever printed, this is the best,' said Michael. 'You've got to give it to them.'

My head began to spin. To Michael (and doubtless *The Enquirer* too) this was just a joke, but to me it was as true as a bananas being yellow. At least I know I'm not imagining things – Prince really is messing with my mind (and has told someone to spread the story) – but where does that knowledge leave me? No one else believes it is true – if I told any of the girls they'd think I was mad

My Secret Diary

(they can't read, so the article would mean
nothing). So now I'm a slave to Prince's whims.

God help me.

Friday 23 June

Shunned the harem last night in favour of an
evening watching re-runs of *Cheers* with Muscles.

We laughed into the early hours, and I didn't
hear so much as a peep from Prince. It seems he
isn't interested in driving me crazy unless it
involves driving women crazy too.

I'd forgotten how much I love Carla from *Cheers*.
Small, tough and feisty, she doesn't take crap from
anyone and really packs her punches (just like me).
She's kinda like a mini-Clint Eastwood with tits
and a bar job (unlike me). From now on, if Prince
tries to mess with me, I'm gonna give him the
extrasensory finger, just like Carla and Clint would.

Saturday 24 June

Carla and Clint are my saviours!

This afternoon, I had a little flirt with Milly and was about to give her a kiss when Prince suggested I did something unspeakably vile (yet admittedly rather appealing). Instead of obeying, I visualised my heroes and told Prince to stick his ideas where the sun don't shine. Bizarrely, I heard my message being spoken in Clint's husky voice ('Get lost, you little pygmy!' chipped in Carla) And – whaddya know? – Prince *apologised*.

What a result.

I'm through with telepathy, and looking forward to being back in the real world.

P.S. Mustn't forget Prince's tips though.

Sunday 25 June

I'm dead. It's official.

Yesterday I was run over and hit by a jeep on

Neverland. It's all over the news. These journalists really do excel with their research. I'm not dead, I'm reading a paper written by people who need to get a life. First Prince, now this – I'm looking forward to being back in the real world.

Monday 26 June

Firmly back in the real world. As real as you can get with Michael around, anyway.

Peter Pan was out in force today – five busloads of kids turned up first thing in the morning, and Michael spent the day acting like a five-year-old. Wherever Michael went, they followed, and I have to say it was a joyous day. I've never seen Michael happier than when he was being pelted by water balloons by 20 screaming children! They were a good bunch too – all from deprived backgrounds and so grateful for the magic of Neverland. I did my bit by doling out the candies. My brandy snaps went down very well, though it was painful for me to resist temptation all day (diet's still going well, and I'm losing weight extra fast now thanks to Jane Fonda's Workout video).

I like kids, but I'm not sure I could handle them every day.

Tuesday 27 June

Another day, another five busloads of children.

I did my best to keep smiling, but all the screaming's starting to grate on me.

Wednesday 28 June

They just keep coming.

I worried I'd go deaf from all the screaming. Left the brandy snaps in the cupboard. Spent the day in the zoo as a regular animal.

Thursday 29 June

Children, children everywhere, and not a minute to think.

Stayed in bed while Peter Pan did this thing. So much for hoping my pet would grow up.

I don't know what to say anymore, nor what to write, for that matter.

1990-2002
The Wilderness Years

I stopped keeping my diary in late 1989, around the time Michael's sister Latoya posed naked for *Playboy*.

Michael had been having such a good time playing Peter Pan all year, but those pictures hit him hard. Personally, I think he was worried people would think it was MJ with a boob job – Latoya and MJ look so similar, after all. Other things were

getting my main man down too: family and friends were asking Mikey for money left right and centre, and he was under pressure to get involved in a Jacksons reunion tour – something he was very against. The more the outside world wanted a piece of him, the more MJ retreated into fantasyland. I was used to his funny ways, and after so many years together felt a deep love for the kindest man I'd ever known.

The fact that I cared so much meant I found it hard to see Michael becoming unhappy. Along with his face, it seemed Michael was slowly beginning to fall apart. I was always there for a hug or a game, but I soon realised there's only so much good just being there for someone can do. (Let's face facts, I was never able to actually speak to and advise Michael, which made consoling just a weeny bit hard!) It was clear to me that my beloved MJ was becoming unwell.

Sure enough, Michael collapsed from nervous

exhaustion in June 1990, and from then on in he needed medical help to get back on his feet. (Mind you, he loved the fact that President Bush and Elton John called him in hospital, bless him.) The docs gave Mike all sorts of pills to help him along, and I offered what I could in the way of brandy snaps and strolls around Neverland, but deep down something had changed between us. Maybe it was just that I felt sad seeing Michael sad. Maybe I could have done more for him.

I'll never know.

What I do know is that the bad times started to outweigh the good. Michael himself pointed that out while we perched on top of his giving tree one day. The only time Michael seemed to be having fun was when he was hanging out with various young people he'd made friends with. Some of them were pretty cool dudes. I'll never forget Macaulay Culkin, the kid from those *Home Alone* movies. One night, Macaulay, MJ and me spent

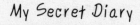

My Secret Diary

hours setting up booby traps, only to realise we were the only ones around to set them off. We were home alone, or so we thought. Little did we know that Uri Geller would pop around the next day, press the doorbell and find himself trapped under 2000 bananas that fell from a net. (Finally, I'd got him back for bending my favourite spoon!)

For a while, I remained in the house, but as Michael spent more and more time with his new friends, I began to feel like a bit of a spare part. Besides, pretending to be interested in playing video games and drinking fizzy pop was difficult when I had five British hotties only a banana's throw away. Increasingly, I found myself tempted away from the house towards more carnal pleasures. I can't be blamed for that – a chimp's gotta do what a chimp's gotta do.

Not that it was all bad for MJ – we hosted Lizzie Taylor's wedding to Larry Fortensky at Neverland in '91 at a cost of – wait for it – $2million.

214

(Muscles dared me to whip off Elton John's toupe, but I didn't.) I was happy for Liz, but it was a difficult day for me, as you can imagine. We could have been great together.

In 2002 the *Dangerous* tour went very well to begin with (though I was very worried about my dear boy flying around those stadiums in a jet pack – I nearly had a heart attack when me and Muscles saw it on the news). Michael was away for a long time, and during that period I did a lot of thinking and really went back to my roots. I spent as much time as possible out of the limelight and down at the zoo being what I am: an animal. There's more to us lot than meets the eye, you know, and I had plenty of lively debates with Louis the llama about the nature of fame and the universe (as separate subjects, you understand). I ended up very fond of Louis – underneath that tough, sneering exterior lies a very delicate and sensitive soul (or as delicate and sensitive as the soul of a creature who

considers fame to be 'a load of bullcrap' and life to
be 'meaningless, frustrating, and ultimately not
worth it' can be). Still, we had some fun, me and
Louis. Being with fellow beasts made me feel more
myself than ever, and I don't think I did one
moonwalk in 1993.

I went back to the house now and again to catch
up with Muscles, who resolutely refused to leave
(giving up *Tarzan* would have killed him) and I'll
never forget watching Michael on *Oprah* saying
Brooke Shields was his girlfriend. I laughed myself
to the floor. Funnier still, Lizzie T came on and said
Michael is the least weird person she's ever known.
The suggestion Michael was normal really got me.

If Liz meant what she said, then I dread to think
what her weird mates were like.

Life was different for me, but good. Michael
seemed as OK as he was ever going to be, and then
it all went horribly wrong. When Neverland was
searched by the police in August 2003, I knew

1990-2002

something was up. A few days later I found out about the accusations against Michael, and I simply didn't believe them. At the same time, I knew in my heart this would be the beginning of the end for him, and my heart sank like never before. Man oh man, did this chimp get the blues. These days it's OK to be honest about such matters, so I've no shame in admitting I became depressed. My banana diet went out of the window, and within a week I was back into the brandy snaps in a big way. Within months I had a $2000 a day habit, and I still wanted more.

The days and nights blurred into one. I ploughed through box after box of snaps, and about a cow's udder-worth of cream a week. When you're addicted to sugar, the outside world begins to lose its meaning. My visits to see Muscles became more about feeding my addiction than spending time with a friend, and I'll always regret the hurt I caused him at times. So often we'd plan a

Tarzan/Lassie double-bill and I'd end up getting
wasted on snaps, shouting obscenities at Cheeta (I
found myself hilarious when 'up' on sugar) until I
crashed into a vile sugar low and burst into tears.
You know how rock stars admit to losing a decade
or more of their lives to cocaine? Well, I did nearly
the same on sugar.

I ballooned, and by the time MJ returned in
pieces from his cancelled tour in November 1993, I
wasn't much use to anyone. I did my best to
console him, but I was fighting my own demons,
and so was he (MJ was popping more pills than
ever to cope with the stress of the accusations).

In the middle of everything, a wonderful event
happened. Michael came home one night and told
me he was all shook up – he'd met a girl. I checked
the date – it wasn't April Fool's day – and asked
him to tell all. He'd met Lisa Marie Presley, and
they had become best friends. Better than that,
they were lovers. I was over the moon. Not only

had Michael found a woman his own age, he was finally doing what grown ups do.

Lisa was so good for him. She encouraged him into rehab and got him to a place where he could face the world again. And then they got married! I was as shocked as the next man, but naturally delighted. Finally, I thought, my manchild's growing up. And take it from me, they couldn't keep their hands off each other.

With Lisa around, the pressure on me to look after MJ was off. A good thing. The bad thing was I had myself to look after, and I wasn't doing a very good job. When my chimpesses moved away to do birthday card work, I was bereaved. All I had left were my brandy snaps, and from 1994 onwards I was in trouble. My mood swings became uncontrollable. I'd go off the rails at the slightest thing, and my attention span was terrible. Believe it or not, I was so strung out that when Prince Michael I was born in 1997, I thought Lisa Marie

was the mother. Little did I know the divorce was through and Michael had married Debbie Rowe (I'd thought she was the new cleaner – turns out she was a nurse).

Paris Michael Katherine came along a year later, and I was overjoyed for Michael. He loved those kids like crazy, and seeing him alive again warmed my soul to the point that I managed to cut back on the brandy snaps and become a 'functioning sugarholic' – to the outside world, I appeared to be OK, but inside I was in turmoil, a slave to my penchant for cream-filled treats.

The other animals knew what was going on, and over time Michael realised too. Even though I had a problem, I was in denial. On several occasions, Michael tried to talk me into rehab, but I wouldn't listen. To be fair to him, he never took my brandy snaps away – he felt it should be my decision to stop. Taking responsibility for my actions was the only way out of this, he would say. Unfortunately, I

chose to continue using, and only took a long hard look at myself when I hit rock bottom.

'Rock bottom' came one fateful September day in 2000. I was waiting for a new shipment of snaps, and highly irritable. Michael brought Prince Michael I over to say 'Hi', but I wasn't in the mood for pleasantries. Prince Michael had brought me a little banana split (he'd made it all by himself, bless him). He handed it over with a smile, but instead of receiving it graciously, I knocked it from his hand and began screaming all manner of obscenities. I'll never forget the way Prince Michael's face went from happy to sad, and I'll forever regret that awful act.

Prince Michael cried, and Michael carried him off. What has become of me? I thought, as they walked away to the house. At that moment, I realised I'd turned into someone I never wanted to be. I was angry, bitter, bored and frustrated, not by my surroundings, but by my addiction.

I began to cry.

Michael came back and I know he could tell I was in pieces. He held me tight, and told me it was all going to be OK. We'd get through this, together. Michael looked me in the eye and I'll be forever grateful for what he said next.

'You're my best friend in the world, Bubbles. I couldn't have wished for a more devoted chimp if I'd tried. We've been through so very much, and I'll never forget all of those magical days we spent together.'

'*Me neither, Pal,*' I said through my tears. '*You don't have a tissue, do you?*'

Maybe it was just a coincidence, but at that moment Michael began to search his pockets. Seconds later, he produced a tissue. He knows me better than anyone, I thought, and perhaps he even understands me.

'*Oh, Michael,*' I said, '*I can't begin to say what these years have meant to me. You're the nicest dude I've*

ever come across. And you're a goddamn weirdo, too!'

At this Michael laughed. Christ, I thought, for this moment only, Michael understands me. *He understands.* I jumped into his arms and tickled him until he begged me to stop. Before we knew it we were both in hysterics.

I was filled with love as I watched Michael laughing with abandon on the ground. What a special, special man, I thought as I smiled. He really is one in a million.

I bet he felt the same way about me.